ALIGN & ACHIEVE

THE COUNTERINTUITIVE APPROACH FOR
HEART-CENTERED ENTREPRENEURS TO
LAUNCH, GROW, AND SCALE THEIR ONLINE
BUSINESS INTO SIX FIGURES WITH STRATEGY,
HEART, AND EASE.

KAMILA GORNIA

PRAISE FOR KAMILA GORNIA

"Kamila has ROCKED my business! I've branded my signature process, my prospects love how I've laid it out AND my free initial consultations have rocked! I follow Kamila's system every time and have gotten a ton of business lately. So thank you!!! I can directly pinpoint it to this process. I've left my job and I'm now LOVING life as a full-time entrepreneur!"

— REBECCA GRUENSPAN, ADOPTION
CONSULTANT

"Kamila is a powerhouse both online and in person. She shares so much value and is incredibly generous with her time, helping each person hash out their biz challenges and leave with a plan of action. Whether it be in a blog post, video or an in person event, Kamila's experience and personality allows her to get her point across, which helps you GET SH*T DONE in your business!"

— LORI STREATOR, BREAKTHROUGH
MIND & BODY

"The content that Kamila provides is absolutely amazing. It has helped me so much in my business and I am only getting started. Her ideas on how to become a content machine are breathtaking. Thank you."

— RACHAEL WOOLLEY, CONFIDENCE COACH

"I just cracked $18K in sales in 30 days. The power of aligned action. I am doing a lot less sales calls but pretty much getting all yes's and I don't even know how to "sell". The only other time I made good money before nearly killed me and I signed a bunch of horrible clients, so this is a truly sweet, sweet victory as this time it feels right and easy."

— EMMA O'SULLIVAN, STRESS COACH

"I realized that just in the first 3 months of THIS year, I am only 4K short from what I made in an ENTIRE YEAR last year. HUGE WIN! I believe SO much of this is contributed to working with Kamila Gornia in various ways over the last year. THANK YOU SO MUCH KAMILA!"

— ELYSE FALZONE, INTUITIVE HEALER

"Joining Kamila's Academy program has been by far the best investment of my life! I was able to leave my 9-5 through this journey in less than 3 months!! Kamila means it when she says got you!"

— MARIAM AZIZ, CONTENT WRITER + STRATEGIST

For more Success Stories, please visit: www.heartbehindhustle.com/success-stories

TABLE OF CONTENTS

HOW TO READ THIS BOOK

Welcome, amazing human.

I am so honored that you have chosen to pick up this book. After serving thousands of entrepreneurs over the years and seeing incredible transformations take place, I now get to share some of the keys to growth with you, too. I've seen people go from zero to creating a thriving authentic online business quickly - experiencing more freedom and joy they ever thought possible, and finally feeling aligned with their vision, values, and personality - now it's your turn.

My goal with the book is to help you step outside of your comfort zone, see your business differently, and really understand the power of aligned strategy and mindset to help you reach ANY goal in business. Whether it's getting your business launched and your first clients booked, or getting to your first $10K month, or scaling to those multiple six figure years, you're in the right place. I've done it all with my clients and I'm going to do my best to share some of the most essential things to help you do the same.

It fills my heart to see entrepreneurs take action, change their lives, and create the exact version of life they've always dreamed of. I never knew it would be possible for me, either. But it was. Now I want to help you do the same, too.

But first - how should you read this book?

Here's a quick guide:

Part 1 is called Alignment Essentials, we will dig into fundamental keys you need to understand in order to create an authentic business that feels great to run and manage. You will discover the dangers behind the usual marketing approaches most "gurus" online tend to tout, and how you can create a rock-solid foundation that sticks for years. This will give you a lot of clarity in your current situation. You may find yourself nodding your head a lot and realizing some things you have been doing in a not-so-ideal way.

Part 2 is where I will share with you an overview of the Aligned Marketing method, my signature methodology for helping our clients create a repeatable marketing system that works powerfully to attract and enroll quality clients into their programs. You will learn one of my secret weapon frameworks to creating effective messaging that converts, as well as the keys we recommend our clients focusing on on a daily basis to get them clients on demand. We will also talk our Aligned Launch process and how we launch our programs into the world. You'll see how get our clients to generate as much as $100K in sales in just 8 weeks and how you can do the same.

And lastly, in Part 3, we will get you to take action on the first and most important step forward. We will talk about what makes offers sell themselves and how to attract the most likely to buy prospects in your business. From there, you will see how you can go from one small action to building massive momentum that will get you to reach six figures faster than you thought possible.

So, you can see, we will be covering a lot. Now a question you might be wondering is:

"Ok Kamila, but why are you doing this?"

I'm going to be completely honest with you. There are three reasons why I wrote this book.

Reason #1 - I'll call this my selfish reason. I did it because I've always wanted to write a book and serve thousands of people to change their lives and grow their businesses, even if they aren't able to invest at a high level in my coaching programs.

Reason #2 - I'll call this my mission-related reason. I did it to get you to stop doing things ineffectively and create an authentic business that truly has the capacity to impact thousands of people's lives. You've been waiting for long enough to do it, and helping you do this is a part of MY mission and the whole reason why I started my company, Heart Behind Hustle®. I believe the more people go after their dreams, the more we get to create a peaceful and loving world.

Reason #3 - I'll call this my business-related reason. I did it that you'll eventually want to hire me and my team to help you implement the strategies you'll learn in this book.

Some people like to do things on their own, whereas others love being able to have access to their mentor, have the ability to ask questions that pertain to their own business, and to accelerate their results by implementing our templates, scripts, and step-by-step strategies that break everything down even more deeply.

So if you read this book and decide you'd like my help in implementing our strategies in your business as quickly as possible, the next step is to watch my free bonus training where you'll learn how to book your first or next 10 clients without feeling guilty for charging what you deserve: **http:// heartbehindhustle.com/bonustraining**

PART I

ALIGNMENT ESSENTIALS

1

VISION INTO REALITY

*I*magine this for a moment:

You wake up in the morning at the exact time your body wants you to wake up. You haven't used the alarm clock in ages and you enjoy being able to listen to your body for guidance instead. You open your eyes and see morning light beginning to stream through the window. The thought of the day ahead fills you with so much excitement and joy. You leap out of bed, smiling, and you go about your morning routine with a clear and calm mind.

You pull out your phone to check notifications. You see a message from a client celebrating a huge breakthrough you've been working on for weeks. The thought of supporting this client in creating this transformation fills you with an immense sense of pride and purpose. You knew she could do this! You look at your other notifications. Another note from a brand new client saying how excited she is for your program to start and that she has been telling all her friends about the work you do. You smile. This isn't uncommon for you. Business has been flowing with complete ease lately, and you can barely believe that this is your life. You respond to your clients and put your phone away. You decide to go for a walk in the park with a delicious latte or tea in hand from a nearby coffee shop. It's your favorite. It feels so good to enjoy each day like this, feeling like a weekend, but it's only Tuesday!

By the time you get home it's late morning and it's time to get to work. You check your email. You had three payments come through. Two from current clients who had been billed for their recurring payments for your program, and one from a new customer for one of your digital products. How fun! You never knew making money could feel so good and so aligned. You show up, you create, you serve your community, you transform your clients... and you are compensated incredibly well for it. In fact, you are bringing in *more than* the amount you've always wanted to bring in. It feels so good to not worry about where your money is coming from anymore. It feels incredible to know that all of your expenses are taken care of, and you have an abundant amount left over for the good things in life.

You go through the planned business activities for the day with complete focus and clarity. You plan out some of your content for the week, you map out your upcoming launch where you'll start enrollment for your new program that you're feeling completely lit up about. And you send out an email to get a few calls booked with amazing people who are desiring to take that next step early. Before the day is over, you already have five calls booked. It feels incredible to know that your business is running like a well-oiled machine, with you showing up in the most inspired way and truly serving your community and clients with heart, integrity, and love. Your clients feel it, too. This is why your calendar gets booked solid anytime you open it up. This is why your programs get sold out. And this is why you continue to crush your financial goals every month. Life is good.

If this feels like an impossible dream, I get it. It can feel unbelievable to know that this can actually be your reality. But what if I told you that you have the power to design the exact type of business and life you've always dreamed of? What if you could actually bring in those call bookings anytime you wanted? What if you could bring in a cash injection in the thousands of dollars, spontaneously? What if you could feel completely filled up with joy about your business? It's possible. And the first step starts right here. Reading this book.

So who is this imaginary person from that story above we just imagined? What if I told you this is pretty much how I feel in my life right now and I have been for years?

Now, I'm not going to lie to you. It's not always easy. There are ups and downs. There are growth pains. And it certainly didn't happen overnight. And of course, there is always the next level to reach and new challenges to overcome. That won't change, in fact, it's to be expected. But truthfully, when I think about my business right now, it honestly blows my mind that I created this. I had no idea something like this was possible. Not to ME. Maybe to other people... never to me.

But yes, I wake up every morning without an alarm clock. I get to have the exact morning I want. I spend some time on my morning routine, and don't usually start working in my business until 10am. Some days are booked with calls for my program or with clients. Others may have some discovery calls on the books. But usually my Mondays and Fridays are completely open and free to do whatever I want. Once a month I do a "conversion" event to create a cash injection in my business, and once a quarter I do a launch for my bigger program to enroll even more clients. This process is simple, repeatable, exciting, and allows me to bring in a nice multiple six figures per year in my business (and has been for years). In fact, this exact business has generated me millions of dollars in revenue over the last several years. I mean, holy cow?! MILLIONS?! ME?!? Never would I have guessed this could be my reality. Never. So if you are feeling unsure about you reaching your big hidden secret dreams... trust me, I know. But what if it truly was possible? What if those wild creative fantasies in your head could be lived out - every day? Working with the perfect clients, living a freedom lifestyle, having ample time for your family and friends, and always having more than enough money. What would that do for you?

The most important thing is that I am not the only one who gets these kinds of results by building an aligned business and creating a marketing plan based on aligned strategic systems. That's the most important part of this whole thing. Before we talk about all the strategies and the good stuff, I really need you to understand the power of what you're about to unfold here. I want to share with you four quick stories from some of our clients to show you what's really possible.

∾

Case Study: Shabana, Relationship Coach

Shabana is an attachment theory focused relationship and dating coach. When she first started working with me in the Academy program, she had been posting on her small Instagram page for a few months sharing her insights about attachment theory. Unfortunately, all of that work has not resulted in any sales. She was feeling a confused and unsure of how to proceed. She thought she was doing everything "right." In fact, even joining the program was a stretch for her since she thought she would have to make some money in her business first before she could invest in getting help. Thankfully, she didn't listen to that voice and took a leap of faith.

Through our process, she realized she had been using social media like an influencer, not like a business owner. Not only was she overloading her audience with random free value, she was training them to expect "free" from her all the time. We had her implement just the first part of our Aligned

Marketing Method (which you'll learn about later in this book) to start turning those lurkers into conversations.

In the program, I taught her the sales flow and she booked her first private client with NO objections. Was it too good to be true? It was so easy. I asked her to make one more tweak to get her into even more conversations and three weeks later she posted in our client group saying she had enrolled 9 more clients with complete ease. That was from the audience she has already built that she thought were NOT buyers. This is the power of the right strategy and the right aligned approach to getting results.

Case Study: Jasmine, Law of Attraction Coach

Jasmine has been an entrepreneur for years. In fact, when we first met on a discovery call in 2014, she wanted help with her jewelry business. She didn't feel ready at that point and she decided to let go of her product based business in lieu of something more purpose driven. Jasmine began listening to her calling of sharing her knowledge of Law of Attraction and manifesting. The problem? She was a full-time mom to a toddler, and didn't have much time to work on the business. While she had a lot of passion and a lot of know-how and success in the business space already, she struggled creating a coaching business that served her lifestyle.

When we began working together, we revamped her business structure to simplify and focus on the people she needed to serve most in the way that would serve her lifestyle most. Instead of selling little tiny courses for a few hundreds bucks (which made her feel resentful) and selling private coaching sessions (which she had no time to do), we creating an aligned six month group program that filled her soul. I helped her launch to her current audience size of just about 1300 people. Weeks later, she had created a $75K revenue launch without any ads. That's compared to her last biggest launch being at about $12K. And the most exciting thing is that we continued to scale this afterwards. Soon after, she reached her goal of generating consistent $30k cash months. That's without running any paid ads. How did she do this?

We listened to what would align best for her vision. She was create the right program at the right price point with the right structure to serve her goals and her lifestyle, and the process of launching felt easy - because she felt so incredibly aligned with it, it felt impossible not to enroll people into the program while following my process and coaching. That's not to say it was effortless, there were ups and downs - there always are. But in the end, it was all worth it and for the first time ever she was able to say: "This feels sustainable."

Case Study: Cindy, Virtual Assistant

Cindy was a virtual assistant whose monthly income was a rollercoaster with zero predictability. She was working with some clients here and there, helping them get stuff done in their business, but the truth is, she was starting to get completely burnt out. She felt like she was working all the time, but yet her income had no consistency. One month she would make $3,000, the next she would make nothing. She wanted to create consistency and flow, without having to work any more hours but had no idea how.

When she started working with me in my program, we had her shift her business model to allow for her to turn her expertise into another way of serving clients. We also realized she had been completely hiding online, lurking in the shadows and expecting clients to come to her and find her, when she wasn't making it easy for them to do so.

The first thing I had her do is build up her confidence and challenge herself to go live on Facebook since that's where most of her ideal clients were hanging out. She was terrified of doing this, she felt so uncomfortable on camera, but knew she needed to do something different. She also had a big vision for her future and knew that hiding would not help her get there. With sweaty palms, she pressed "Go Live" and showed up. Even though she only had three people watch her live, she did it anyway. She thought, at least this is practice. And to her surprise, she landed a paying private client from that first live! That was the moment she really saw the power of authentic visibility.

The next thing we did was change her business model to minimize her working with service clients and had her create a group program so she could teach her skills and knowledge to people in a new way. She went through my launch process and ended up getting her program completely sold out, enrolling 8 ideal clients (when her goal was 5!) in just a few weeks. This is someone who did NOT have a traditional community of her own! She did not have her own Facebook group, email list, or an Instagram page.

Soon after, Cindy was able to stabilize her income at a recurring $5K+ cash months, and she went from being terrified of showing up online into being a total content creation expert, public speaker, and visibility maven.

Case Study: Rachel, Tarot Reader

Our last case study in this section is Rachel, who began working with me in the Academy as a tarot reader. The industry standard in the tarot reading, intuitive, and healing space is that you typically sell your readings/sessions separately and at a low cost, often under $100. We've had many people like Rachel in my programs and this is always the first mindset block to overcome. Despite having a magnetic personality, Rachel struggled with building her audience and converting followers into sales at a repeatable and consistent way.

We had to get her to start thinking like an entrepreneur and following our process rather than listening to the "industry standard." First, we shifted her marketing model to make the flow of people converting into paying sessions increase. Then, we had her implement a process to turn those single sessions into longer term paying clients that would receive a combination of tarot reading, intuitive guidance, and coaching to help them with their transformation. Within three months, Rachel made enough money to quit her day job and was able to focus on her business full time!

A few months after that, she had her first $10k month and is now working with clients in group programs, serving her community, and thriving in her passion-driven business.

I COULD GO on and on with testimonials and case studies, but you can take a look for yourself on our website by going to our training page here: **http://heartbehindhustle.com/bonustraining**

And here's the thing. These entrepreneurs were

able to create incredible aligned results in their businesses not because they were lucky, not because they had a huge budget to spend on ads, and not because they were special in any particular way that's different from you and me. They did it because they built a business utilizing the principles you'll discover in this book and in our programs.

I'm so honored and thrilled to be able to share that with you, too. Over the following chapters, we'll be setting the foundation for understanding why this process works so well and how you can start actually implementing it in your business, too. Get ready for a fun ride!

2

WHO THIS MESSAGE IS FOR

*I*t was August 2015. I was standing in the middle of a big room during a business conference cocktail party in Chicago, gripping my Jameson and Ginger tightly, half-hoping no one notices me and half-wishing someone would come talk to me to ease my nerves.

I've been in business for about a year at that point and I've had my fair share of networking events I've attended (most of them fueled with liquid courage) but this was the first I've attended alone, without a buffer biz wingwoman. Plus, this one was happening in the middle of the day and was going to be followed up with two more keynotes I wanted to attend, so drinking more than one cocktail felt weird.

To top it all off, this event was more of a "super-profesh and official-looking / buttoned-up" kind of business conference, so I was surrounded by older white men in suits, and classy middle aged women wearing Gucci and diamonds.

And here I was, standing in my little black dress that felt too tight, high heels that were rubbing the backs of my feet raw each time I moved, and hair that was once straight, now pouffy and frizzy from the humidity outside.

What the hell was I even doing here?

I noticed a girl closer to my age standing by the bar. She seemed to be alone, but not nearly as uncomfortable as I was. I took a swig of my drink, straightened out my dress, and headed over to say hello.

"Oh my god, maybe I'll finally make a friend who understands and we can laugh this whole thing off. OH! Maybe she'll be my business bestie! I've heard people talk about those all over social media, it'd be great to have a local friend whom I can meet up with to talk business. Fingers crossed..."

"Hey! It seems like we're in the same industry. Marketing, right?" I pointed out the yellow colored name card stranger-girl had on her tailored black top.

"Yeah, you too right? What do you do?" She replied.

"I'm a marketing strategist. I help entrepreneurs get out there online so they can get seen, get paid, make an impact... I mostly focus on Facebook ads and sales fu-"

"Oh really? I'm a marketing strategist too. You have an MBA?" She cut me off.

"No... but I've been in business for about a year and have been doing marketing for —"

"Oh yeah, see... I have an MBA." She looks me up and down slowly with judging eyes. "I started my agency recently but I have my sights set for some great big clients. Good luck with your business.... girl." She smiled sarcastically, grabbed her martini, and walked away.

I stood there, shocked.

"What the hell just happened? First of all, what the actual F? Second of all, who does she think she is? Third of all, this event is clearly not my scene." I downed my drink, grabbed my bag, and called an Uber with shaky hands.

Because, in that moment all of my suspicions had been confirmed....

I clearly didn't belong in this business world. What was I even thinking?

As a young, immigrant, then-25-year old woman without a "real" (read: brick and mortar) business, I was already feeling uncomfortable. I didn't have an MBA. I didn't have a million dollar business. I didn't have investors, or benefactors, or even any saved up money to invest in a big start. I didn't have an office with a physical location. I didn't have employees, nor did I want any.

To traditionally-minded business people, all of that resulted in dismissive glances, and "oh how cute" snickers about how millennials like me are such dreamers and "hopefully she has a real job too, poor thing."

What these people did not know was that I had started online marketing at the age of 12. What they didn't know was this was my third profitable business, second of which was fully online. What they didn't know is that I sold my previous business without any prior experience. What they didn't know was that I was already at six figures in revenue even though I had started my business just 14 months prior. What they also didn't know was that I left my day job because I was able to fully support myself on my business income, without going into debt, and without selling my soul.

Unfortunately, at the time, I didn't realize this about myself either. I'd always had a bad habit of judging myself too harshly. I wanted to be liked and accepted by everyone, and this meant I could never measure up to my unrealistic expectations of myself.

I was simply never good enough.

Being 25 years old, I thought I wasn't experienced enough. As a woman, I thought I wasn't strong enough. As an introvert, I thought I wasn't charismatic enough. As an immigrant, I thought I wasn't eloquent enough. As a millennial, I thought I wouldn't be taken seriously enough. As an online business owner, I thought it meant I wasn't "legit" enough. Having "only" gotten my Bachelor's degree, I thought I wasn't qualified enough. Being "only" at six figures, I thought I wasn't successful enough. You get the picture.

Not enough. Not enough. Not enough.

If you're anything like me, you've felt that feeling of "not enoughness" before too. Or perhaps, if you're like some of my clients, for you it's about being TOO MUCH. Too loud, too quiet, too weird, too quirky, too brash, too polite, too serious, too nerdy...

I understand how it feels. I understand how easy it is for you to get in your head, hold yourself back from expressing your true authentic self, and hoping people don't notice you while at the same time *praying* that they do. It's confusing! How can you want to be noticed and NOT want to be noticed at the same time?

How can you want to be successful but be terrified of it at the same time? How can you desire to build a thriving business but hesitate when doing the work or learning the steps to take? How can you think about your passion and potential all day long but never take action on it?

You aren't broken. There's nothing wrong with you. YOU ARE ALREADY COMPLETE AND WHOLE. But until YOU realize that and believe that, nothing I say will change how you feel about yourself.

"Not enough" or "too much" has no room in leadership and business.

If you want to make the income and the impact to match your potential, things have to change. And no, it has nothing to do with the events you go to, or the people you interact with, the business you run, or the degrees you do or don't have.

It has to do with *you*. Yes, *YOU* are the cornerstone of all of it. And how you manage and run YOU will affect more than just your income and your impact, it affects your entire LIFE.

Because first of all, you have to stop feeling sorry for yourself. Second, you have to make a DECISION that you're ready to make a change. And third, you have to step into leadership and take ACTION already! Because what you do here on this earth? It's *bigger* than you. It's time to claim some responsibility. And I'm gonna help you do it.

So this book is a perfect fit for you if you're a brand new entrepreneur, trying to find your way. It's a great fit if you've been in business for years but seem to feel stuck and stagnant. It's a great fit if you're exploring your options, or want to get your butt kicked, or want to start doing things in a much more aligned way for you.

So if all of that sounds good? Let's begin.

3

THE TRUTH ABOUT ALIGNMENT
AND FINDING CLARITY

*S*o this book is all about understanding how to successfully align yourself with what you want so you can achieve it, plus tactical strategies to help you get there.

But in order for us to have an effective conversation about this, let's start the beginning. What is "alignment" anyway?

Well, in the world of entrepreneurship the word "alignment" is coming up pretty frequently - especially lately as people are more and more interested in creating a business that works FOR them and not the other way around.

When I talk about alignment, which is often, I see it as being put on the right path *for you*. A path that feels right in respect with your goals, vision, personality, and more. It's a deep inner knowing that things are adding up, they are all building up to something you desire to see. Whether it's opportunities all of the sudden becoming unlocked, whether it's receiving clarity on something you were confused about before, or whether it's performing the activities to help you reach your desired outcome in a better, faster, or easier way. Alignment can mean a lot of different things to a lot of different people.

There are, however, some things people tend to misunderstand about the concept of alignment.

Thing #1: Being aligned does NOT mean you are doing things that are EASY.

Aligned and easy are NOT synonyms. In fact, doing the aligned thing is often not easy at all. It may be challenging because in order for you to reach your desired outcome you will have to get outside the comfort zone - and everything outside of the comfort zone IS meant to be uncomfortable. So, it can feel uncomfortable AND aligned at the same time.

However, often when you do the aligned action, you may notice that things will begin to flow for you a lot sooner. Or perhaps you will end up reaching your goals faster than you realized. Or perhaps the universe will somehow give you signs that you ARE on the right track and you should keep going. It will give you that feeling on being on the right track. That's alignment.

Thing #2: Being aligned does NOT look the same for everyone.

This is another common misconception. Just because something feels aligned for you (for example, showing up on live video for your visibility every day) does not mean that it will feel aligned for someone else. There are SO many ways for you to hit your goals online and for you to create a repeatable marketing system, such as the Aligned Marketing Method we will teach you in this book. The tactics and vehicles will change, however, based on what feels the most aligned for your personality.

My goal here is not to push ONE specific way for you to do things. Yes, it's true that some tactics work better than others. But ultimately, the best strategy is one that you can do consistently and that feels GOOD for you to do. Not one that you think you *have* to do because everyone else is doing it, even though it feels like you are absolutely going against everything you believe in when doing it.

Thing #3: Discomfort or lack of skill/practice in something does NOT mean you are out of alignment.

This is a biggie. Sometimes I'll have a student that comes to me saying they refuse to do sales calls. They just won't do it. They are introverted, they are worried about being salesy or pushy, they tried before and failed, whatever. That's fine. Not everyone has to do sales calls. However, there are some key frameworks that tend to work REALLY well for growth in business when utilizing sales calls. A lot of people mistake their lack of skill or lack of practice in the art of sales, for example, as being out of alignment with doing sales at all. When in fact, they simply haven't found the right way to DO sales so it can feel easier.

The truth is, if you are an entrepreneur you WILL have to do sales. There is no way around it. Sure, once you've grown enough you will be able to hire sales-people to help you. But in order to get there? You will have to do it yourself. So what can you do? Instead of giving up, treat it like any new skill you have to learn.

I see this like losing weight or getting fit. You will not get fit and grow muscles in one session at the gym. I wish it were that easy. It takes weeks, months, if not years to build the kind of body you see on Instagram. If you go to the gym expecting to get that in a week (when you're far away from that goal right now), you're setting yourself up for failure. Now, if REACHING that goal feels aligned... Guess what? The PROCESS gets to feel aligned too - as soon as you a find way to do it consis-tently in a way you can learn to enjoy and as soon as you turn it into a habit and a challenge, not something that you have to get right the first time around.

Thing #4: You are allowed to change your mind.

Your business will go through a constant evolution. You as an entrepreneur will also go through many evolu-tions and versions of yourself. That also means that what you find aligned right now might not feel aligned later. There's nothing wrong with you, it doesn't mean you aren't focused enough or that you're confused. You are allowed to change your mind and evolve.

This actually brings me to the next point I wanted to cover separately - the topic of clarity. This is the most misunderstood concept and it's causing SO many entrepreneurs to stay stuck. I don't want that to be you.

What's the REAL deal with gaining clarity?

One of the most common things I hear from my students goes something like this: "I can't move forward because I don't have clarity on ___ yet."

We need to talk about this, because it seems like we all think that clarity is something that just one day appears out of thin air. And yeah, sometimes it can. It's not uncommon for us to sometimes be just doing something totally random, like taking a shower or talking a walk in the park, where a brilliant flash of an idea comes in, giving you that yummy feeling of clarity. Now to take action! Yeah, that sounds fantastic. And because you've experienced that once (or many times) before, you think that in order for you to take ANY action, you need to wait for that flash of brilliance to come in. But like... when will it? Will it come today? Tomorrow? Next week? Next year?

And the question I really want you to ask yourself is, what if it never comes? Are you ok with never taking action? Are you ok with staying exactly where you are right now? Are you ok with living the exact life you're living right now and never going forward with reaching your dreams?

Here's the thing you need to understand: You do NOT need to have complete clarity in order to be successful in business.

I know, right? Maybe that sounds a bit counterintuitive. After all, isn't the first step in all the business courses always to get clarity? Yes. I'm not saying going into growing your business completely blind is the answer. It's not. AND you get to grow even if you aren't clear on every single part of your business.

Here's what I know and teach my clients all the time: **Clarity comes from ACTION, not overthinking.**

I used to fall for this mistake all the time. I felt like in order to move forward, I needed to get completely clear on my offer, on who I serve, on my brand, my website, all the details. In the meantime, I kept changing my mind. One day, I felt excited about helping one type of person, and the next I had a totally different idea. The thing is, you are a creative multi-dimensional being with loads of ideas. The ideas will never stop. So even once you think you have clarity, that might be short-lived anyway. So what do you do? You take action anyway. What we want you to do is get ENOUGH clarity to move forward and then take the action necessary to grow.

Here's a fun fact. I started my coaching business in 2014 as a life coach because I honestly had no idea who I wanted to serve and how. I just showed up and did what I thought I wanted to do. As I worked with each client, I got clearer and clearer about what felt good and not so good about each experience. Did I like when the client cried about their family life? Did I like when they asked me questions about business? Did I feel excited to talk about how I organize my finances? Did I feel like I could talk forever and ever about how to build confidence when it came to marketing? What got me excited (and not so much) came from me actually being in the weeds of my business - NOT from thinking about it! This is how I ended up calling myself a marketing strategist. I realized I LOVED talking about marketing with my clients and I did not want to talk about other things. It was my sweet spot. As I grew my business, I began getting even more excited about the bigger picture - the whole business and sales, not just marketing. So I started calling myself a business coach. My business went through numerous evolutions, one spearheading the next naturally, not forcefully. It was all an organic transformation that only could have happened by the pure act of doing and first-hand experience. Clarity? Clarity did not come for YEARS. Even now there are pieces of my business I do not have complete clarity in. This is exactly why I hire mentors, coaches, and join programs to help me overcome this. I then learn, take action, and figure things out as I'm in the weeds of it once again.

I have made millions of dollars in revenue WITHOUT having complete clarity on every piece of my business. Think about that. If I can do that, why are YOU waiting for 100% clarity right now? And what could YOU do if you just got started NOW? What if you could just start with what you DO know and trust that the rest will come at the right aligned time for you? What if by doing so, you could reach five figures of sales in the next few weeks? What if you ended the year reaching your goal income? That won't happen by itself, but it can once you start taking action and doing the damn thing! I hope you can feel how passionate I am about this.

Alright, let's keep moving forward.

4

THE THREE PROBLEMS OF THE ONLINE BUSINESS INDUSTRY

I've been in the online space since 2002 when I created my first hobby venture, but for more focused business reasons starting 2009. In that time, I've seen a lot of trends come and go, and a lot of habits entrepreneurs have adopted that have supported or thwarted their growth.

Since everything we teach our clients is based on integrity, alignment, and acting from the place of love, I wanted to bring some common concerns that are prevalent in this online industry you're stepping into (or already playing in) and how we can ensure you don't fall into these traps yourself.

Problem #1: Overpromising and underdelivering

Pretty much every single launch I do, I speak with some people who have been burned by other coaches or trainers before. They either paid for something that was not delivered, the person they hired ghosted them, or they simply felt ignored as soon as that relationship changed from a "prospect being sold to" to a "client in the program."

This honestly breaks my heart. And unfortunately it's not uncommon in our space. Now, I want to be clear I am not talking about those few students who buy a program, don't do the work or give up after a barely trying, and then cry about it because it didn't magically fix their life. That doesn't necessarily mean the program was bad, it usually means that the student wasn't committed enough to doing the work. Creating more commitment from students is easily fixable, but you also have to remember that as a business owner, people not following through is rarely your fault. After all, you can't show up knocking at people's doors telling them to do the work, right? That's totally not scalable. However, there are things you can do to encourage engagement. We won't talk about that in this book, but just know, there are solutions to this problem.

What I am talking about here are people who are GREAT at marketing and selling but TERRIBLE at delivering on their promises. Whether the program they sold was actually a bait and switch and the students are now not learning what they were told they'd learn, or they are getting completely irrelevant and outdated information that doesn't work anymore, or they are not getting access to their promised purchase and are unable to contact support for help when it was promised as a part of the agreement. All of these things are icky, sleazy, and DEFINITELY a big no-no.

How can you avoid falling into this trap?

To stay in integrity, we want to ensure you have your heart in the right place. Do you actually want to help people? I know you want to make money, but are you as committed to helping others as you are to making a great life for yourself? Are you willing to continue educating yourself so you can create the best trainings for your students? Are you willing to show up for your clients as promised? Are you committed to the results of your clients by giving them everything they need to succeed? This is ESPECIALLY important if you charge high ticket prices.

Now, if you're new in business I know there might be a little thought that's coming up now: "But I'm new! I haven't worked with any clients yet. How can I promise them ANYTHING? I have nothing to show for what I can do, except my passion and drive. Isn't that enough?"

It is. If you follow through with it. The truth is, the more you work with clients, the more you stay immersed in your industry and continue to improve on your skills, the more you are committed to your clients and listening to them and seeing how you can help them reach their goals - the more you WILL start to see results for your clients, too. And once you do? You can charge more.

Your "newness" is actually a great thing AS LONG as you follow through with running the business to break through this place of being new. As long as you genuinely want to help people and you actually care. If that's the case? Great. Your pricing will be aligned to your level of experience, you will go through the steps necessary to gain the social proof to charge more, build out your methodology, and scale from there. It all starts with your heart.

So, do you want to genuinely help? Do you enjoy seeing a transformation happen for them? Do you draw fulfillment from knowing that the work you've done with someone has actually changed their life? If so, you'll do just fine.

Core lesson: Don't ever guarantee results. Don't promise the world if you can't (or haven't been able to) deliver. Set realistic expectations but keep the clients' vision clear and high. Get clear on what is truly possible for them, and don't do any of that bait and switch nonsense.

Cool? Ok, great. Let's continue.

Problem #2: High-Pressure Sales

This one is a biggie and a huge reason why many heart-centered entrepreneurs struggle with sales themselves. I've spoken with countless students about their previous experiences with sales people. I've heard how some people were manipulated and pressured to buy the advertised program even though they've already said a firm no. I've heard how people were *bullied* about their decision to say no. They were told to take out a loan, get a new credit card, find a loan shark, whatever -

when it was clear the person was not in the right place to do so (plus, they already said NO THANKS!).

It's no surprise you might be worried about learning sales and not wanting to appear salesy. After experiences like that? No wonder! If it takes being a pushy sleazeball to get clients, count me out!

Here's the thing: Guilting, bullying, pressuring, and manipulating people to buy is absolutely NOT ok. But yet many people do it because they think the only way to get sales is to be a "hardcore closer" and salesperson. It's what a LOT of sales experts teach!

To be clear, if someone wants to do these things (use a credit card, etc) to join your program, that's frankly their decision and none of your business. I will sometimes get a new credit card to enroll for a program because I like to take advantage of reward points or cash back for big purchases and 0% APR. But, what is NOT ok is being told you aren't serious enough or committed enough or that you will never succeed unless you sign up for a program when you know you aren't ready for it (or just don't want it). It's NOT ok to to be sold that if you aren't willing to take out yet another credit card to pay for a program then you must not love yourself enough or have mindset problems.

It's NOT okay to take away someone's choice. And it's NOT ok to make people feel bad for making a decision when that decision didn't work for their agenda. But yet, many sales training programs I've seen teach this exact thing.

Here are some things I've heard from sales experts:

👿 "Don't let the person off the phone until they say yes."

👿 "If they don't want to buy, tell them they must not want it (their results) bad enough. If their kid was dying, they'd find the money for treatment. So they can find the money for your program, too."

👿 "If they don't want to buy because of price, tell them if they don't buy they will fail or will never succeed. If they can't afford it, they have mindset problems and are doomed to fail - unless they buy your program. Then they will succeed."

That is true barf city. Here's a personal experience: I remember recently getting on the phone with someone to explore potentially working with them. On the call, I got a gut feeling that told me this is not the right fit for me right now, so I told them no, not right now. They did not let me off the phone after that for like 20 minutes. I should have probably just hung up but maybe I'm too nice *shrug*.

And look, yes I know overcoming objections is important. You need to learn it and not shy away from it. HOWEVER, there's a big difference between overcoming objections to guide and help the person make the best decision FOR THEM (not just for you) when they clearly aren't SURE about the decision or are hesitating (but might want to join)... versus those who flat out confidently say "No thanks."

If you've been burned by bad experienced in the

past with coaches or experts, or feel resistant to selling and worried about appearing "salesy" because you don't resonate with the whole pressure sales approach that almost every sales guru teaches, ***don't worry.***

You do NOT have to pressure ANYONE to get them to work with you.

In fact, in my business I operate under a strict "no convincing" policy. This means I refuse to CONVINCE anyone to want to work with me, period. Convincing just takes too much work, energy, and drains my soul and I honestly don't want to do it. Some people might say that makes me a "bad" sales person. Others might say it's because I have "mindset issues." But I have successfully generated millions of dollars in revenue in my own business WITHOUT sacrificing my values, so I think my approach is working out just fine. *shrug*

When I tell my clients they don't have to convince, pressure, or persuade anyone to work with them, they often tell me how much of a sigh of relief that is. But it's true!

Imagine that selling could feel natural, enjoyable, and fun - not just for you but for the other person involved. Imagine them truly connecting with you, and you with them. You're in business to HELP people, to serve them, to make an impact. Sales need to be a part of that. When you learn the right way to do sales, it gets to feel beautiful and impossible not to do.

What if getting off a sales conversion, the new client was to tell you "THANK YOU for selling this to me!" Or "This was SUCH a great conversion, I am so excited to work with you!" Isn't that SO much better of an experience? It's uplifting not just for your clients but for YOU, too!

Imagine sales being a natural extension of service. Imagine it feeling like a beautiful conversation, an unleveling feeling that rises up and reaches their heart and yours. How beautiful. If you want to do things this way, YOU GET TO. Glad you're here. Let's keep going.

Problem #3: Perfectly Aspirational

Two of these elements are important to address: 1) the deep and often subconscious desire to make everything perfect, which is often driven by comparison. And that comparison is frequently driven by aspirational marketing which actually draws us in. So let's start with marketing.

When done right, it truly gets to feel amazing, plus it helps the right people get amazing results that improve their lives. Win-win! The problem? When people severely exaggerate their own results, unrealistically amplify how great their life is, and focus on promising and guaranteeing their clients the wins and riches, too - but without any depth to it. "Here I am with my mansion, five Lambos, a yacht, and a horde of half naked girls drinking expensive champagne out of the bottle. I'm so cool and popular and rich, don't you wanna be like me? Buy my course!"

Now, don't get me wrong. There's nothing wrong with having a lavish lifestyle if that's what you desire. Heck, who wouldn't want to have a nice car and a big house? And if I could drive my dream car, I obviously would do it in a heartbeat (I know you would, too!). But if your ONLY claim to fame is how popular and rich you are (especially when it's exaggerated) and NOT how you can help people overcome their problems and challenges? There's something not quite right. This is often when we see these claims of "How I make 8 figures in 8 weeks, and here's how you can, too!". They're selling a dream that feels impossible but they say if you buy that program, you will have it, too. But, like... Will you? REALLY? Just one 6-week course to make 8 figures when you're starting at zero? Come on. First of all, I call BS. Second of all, it's going back to this problem of overpromising and underdelivering. Third, it's illegal. FTC will be knocking on your door if you do this. And fourth, just because one person was successful with something, doesn't mean they can help others achieve that same result. So when you see these amazing lifestyles, dig a little deeper. How did they make this money? Is all that stuff you're flaunting ACTUALLY theirs or did they rent it for the photo-shoot? Is there any real depth or substance to what they are selling or is it just about "be like me"? You get to be the judge of that.

There's another version of "aspirational" marketing that's more subtle. You've seen it. Pictures in front of the Eiffel Tower, wearing gorgeous Ted Baker dresses, perfectly blown out hair, professionally done makeup in every photo, kissing the love of their life in one picture while drinking champagne and eating maca-roons in another. Touting a completely perfect lifestyle with absolutely zero mistakes ever made, no challenges experienced, and a life to drool over that's like straight out of a Disney movie.

Again, it's not about living an amazing lifestyle that's the problem. Who doesn't want that? It's about using the lifestyle as the ONLY thing that you have going for you that's the problem and NOT the things you can help others with. So, making your marketing more about you and less about them. Which is a big mistake.

Cause what happens then? People buy your products, they don't get the same results ("Hey I'm still trying to make ends meet and my trip to Paris feels like a VERY distant future! I haven't even gotten a client yet! What's wrong with me?!), and then they feel like it's their fault for not getting there.

Hear me loud and clear right now: it is NOT your fault. It's very easy to fall in love with the dream. The problem comes up when the dream is sold and the system to get there does NOT match up. That in itself is misaligned and inauthentic to the integrity of your offer and promise. So if you've bought courses or programs like this before and didn't get results, it's not your fault. Some people are great at marketing but not as great at the delivery. Ending up overpromising and underdelivering. Big no-no. We talked about this already.

I want to let you know if you've ever experienced this, it's not your fault and there ARE people out there who actually know how to get people results. When looking at someone to hire and whose program to join, make sure you actually check that they have worked with clients, they have gotten results for people, and their "perfect" lifestyle isn't their only claim to fame. Unless, of course, they're honest about it and don't pretend to be perfect at all. Authenticity rules!

There's a way to communicate the promise of your offer that's big AND believable (so people actually *want* it) while staying in integrity with you being able to actually deliver on that promise. That's what we'll want you to do. More on that later.

So what's the real impact of all of this? Well, it's actually pretty huge and it affects a LOT of entrepreneurs without them realizing it. Like I said already, there's a common trend in successful coaches, influencers, and business owners flaunting their life on social media and painting this idealistic version of life that has zero flaws, faults, or challenges. All you have to do is go on Instagram for a minute to find pictures of lifestyles, bodies, or toys to drool over. Now, of course, part of that is marketing. There's nothing wrong with painting the vision of what's possible. After all, we're all in this world of growth and personal development. It's great to remind ourselves that reaching this level of success is a possibility and to be surrounded by greatness and what motivates us.

However, seeing people always showing up SO perfect and put together all the time, this actually ends up putting a LOT of pressure on new entrepreneurs and sets the wrong expectations for what it REALLY looks like behind the scenes. This causes that desire to be perfect, to do everything right, so you can feel worthy of living a great life, too. So you'd spend way too much time on creating the perfect plan, crafting the perfect message, designing that perfect Instagram feed, and waiting for the perfect time to launch when you're feeling fully ready. Because, after all, once everything is perfect, there's no way it can fail, right? There's no way someone can dislike it or reject you, right? Mmm... Not quite.

Perfectionism is a big challenge because it encourages you to keep procrastinating on the things that actually matter and will impact your audience - simple things like showing up and doing the thing you really want to do, whether it's coaching, consulting, writing, whatever. So you keep waiting to show up. Keep waiting to put that offer out there. Because it's not as fancy as So-and-So's yet. Their sales pages are perfect. They get so much engagement. Their website is gorgeous. They look stunning in their photoshoots. And then you look at your own business and it's hard not to feel discouraged. After all, how can you possibly compete?

So as you can see, this one is a big and intertwined problem. People you follow show up with a perfect life, they do everything perfectly (mostly because they have a TEAM that does it for them), they are successful, and then you assume in order to ALSO be successful your level of quality or marketing or design or whatever has to match theirs - which of course is gonna be hard to do if you're new or don't have a team or a huge budget... and then that makes you feel like you're not going to grow or succeed, and then you feel bad about yourself, and then you spiral and stop and hide.

So what to do here? Bottom line: Just be aware of what content you consume. It is 10000% ok to consume aspirational content as long as it motivates and inspires you and DOES NOT make you feel unworthy or undeserving of success. It's ok to follow influencers or coaches online who have an amazing life that you wish you could have as well, as long as you REMEMBER that their life is not without its faults too - whether they talk about them or not. No one is perfect. And that's a good thing for you. People are STARVED for relatability. NOT being perfect is an advantage. People get to resonate with you and relate to you. You are just like them. That's a big pro!

There are people who have enrolled in my Academy program, which is a high ticket program, BECAUSE they felt like me showing up as authentically me, not making a fuss over things, just sharing and helping and training without the need to make things super fancy or complicated, was actually inspiring to them. It made them feel like maybe if I can make money just being myself and doing things simply, they can do that too. I show up on livestreams for my programs without makeup, super casual, and just ready to help people. That's how I am. And that's who resonates with me. And sometimes I dress up and look pretty, and sometimes I'm just natural. And guess what? I get to be successful no matter what. What you need to remember is that YOU are worthy and deserving of success NO MATTER what you look like, what your situation is, whether you're techy or not, whether you have a team of a big budget, whether you feel ready or not yet. YOU GET TO CREATE THE EXACT ALIGNED LEVEL OF SUCCESS YOU DESIRE. Today. Now. It's happening already. You are DOING. Feel that. Believe that. Own that. It's already happening for you.

You're doing great <3

With me? Let's keep going.

5

BIG RESULTS WITH TINY AUDIENCES

*I*f you had told me years ago that I didn't need a big audience to make good money, I would have laughed in your face. I've been building audiences online since 2002. I thought that creating the biggest audience possible was the key to success. Not just financially but also emotionally. After all, that's what everyone told me! So I believed that if I had an audience I'd finally feel worthy. I'd finally deserve love. I'd deserve to feel happy.

I know, it sounds kind of messed up. But I really believed that for the longest time. I needed that reassurance from external sources to tell me that I am on the right path, that I am doing well. When I started my healthy food blog in 2012, it really fed me even more. I'd share vulnerably about my experience with dieting, attempting to lose weight and the challenges I'd experienced. I shared recipes I recreated for the blog and I'd get so much engagement from people who felt connected to me. It drove me. It made me feel so good.

In a difficult time in my life, it also made me feel less alone.

Anyway, about a year into my blog business I started making money through brand deals and sponsorships. It was the first time I had ever started making money 100% online. It was super cool. After a while though, I wanted to take this deeper. I asked myself: Would I be able to actually make money outside of brand deals? How could I take it to the next level? I already had 100,000 people who were visiting my blog every single month, but between brand deals and sponsorships I was only bringing in maybe $2k-$3k per month, which is definitely not enough to comfortably live on. So what would I do? I figured that an easy next step would be creating a digital product. I saw many people online doing this already so I figured - it must be super effective. So, I put together some of my best recipes and created some brand new ones. I put it all into a pretty recipe PDF and tried selling it to my audience.

Results? Abysmal. I made exactly zero dollars. Like literally, the only sale that came in was from myself... testing the process to make sure it was working. 😄

Granted, I had no idea how to do an effective launch or create a sales strategy (my background was in marketing, not sales), but man. Zero sales with an audience of this size?! How brutal is that? 100K people visited my website every month. I mean, holy cow?! And not a SINGLE person wanted to buy my stupid $5 ebook? How could I not feel disappointed and embarrassed? What a complete flop.

Fortunately, being the driven 23 year old, at the time, I figured this must not be the key. So I carried on. Eventually, I came across a business course that taught me the essential sales foundations I was missing (that made my blog business flop in terms of actual sales) and I also learned what I can do to couple my skills in marketing and audience building WITH sales psychology. I also hired my first long-term business coach who had me do some pretty uncomfortable things. I'm so glad I worked with her. I had so many sabotaging thoughts that were holding me back, it's surprising I ever had any results.

- "I'm smart, I should be able to figure this out on my own"
- "I have a background in marketing, how hard can it be to build a real business?"
- "But I already know what to do, there must be some magic secret I'm missing! I have to figure it out."

I had this whole notion that a bigger audience MUST mean more success. And sure, sometimes it can help (if built correctly). But when I decided to pivot and I began learning about the magic of online SALES and building an online service based-business instead, back in 2014, I began to notice some things. People who were JUST starting out, with NO audience at all, were making more money than I was with an audience of thousands of people. How was that possible?

I was always good at building audiences, but it took

a while for me to learn how to sell to them. I was NOT a natural sales person. It made me so uncomfortable. Everyone I learned sales from was teaching a pretty pressure based approach and it never felt aligned for me, but it was the only method I knew at the time. I wanted to be a good student so I learned and did it. (Thankfully, I later revamped the whole process and LOVE selling now. And if you're worried about having to be all pushy on sales calls, don't worry - you DO not have to be AT ALL! But more on that later.)

Through all of these experiences, I decided to make a change. I thought to myself:

> *"What if it was possible for me to make ALL the money I want WITHOUT having to build a huge audience at all? What if I focused on the things that ACTUALLY bring me money, rather than just doing the things I thought I "should" do?"*

So I tried it. I stopped worrying about generating thousands upon thousands of subscribers to my email list just for the sake of vanity or growth. I stopped attaching my sense of worth so much to that number of followers on my social media. I stopped posting on social media 5 times a day and instead, I started creating better quality content that I posted more sparingly. I stopped TRYING so much and started BEING PRESENT with my audience. I listened deeply. I heard what they were saying and asking for. I catered my work to HELP them. To make them actually grow. And you know what? It felt REALLY good. It felt so aligned, so authentic, and so natural to just BE there with my audience, to show up without overthinking and just create.

Before I realized it, my business skyrocketed. I went from making maybe $1k-$3k per month in my marketing coaching business to $15k-$30k months pretty quickly. Best of all? I've sustained my five figure months for years without stopping. I have consistently generated five figure months, upwards of $48k cash in a single month, for five straight years in a row at the time of writing this book. But the most amazing thing is that I did it WITHOUT all the things I thought I had to do or have.

So now I want to bring this to you...

One of the biggest concerns I hear from people is about building an audience. People think that they need to build a list first before making sales. They think that the bigger the audience, the more profitable their business. So they focus on all the wrong things in the beginning (like I did) and then they STILL struggle. Let me ask you this:

Would you rather have an audience of 10,000 people who refuse to buy anything you sell... or an audience of 1,000 who ADORE you, see you as a leader, and buy your stuff no matter what price they are?

Yeah this is a silly question, I know. But the reality is, that when you put the RIGHT tools into practice, you do NOT need a huge audience to grow. Especially when you sell services, private coaching, or group programs. Especially when you do things in a way that is connected.

A few quick examples:

My client, Cara, made $100K in cash in 6 months of us working together with an audience she said was "dead" and "filled with the wrong people." Well, she pivoted and shifted her energy and offers and made bank to her list of 1000 people.

My client, Rachel, got to $10K months by stepping into more confident selling of her tarot sessions AND adding in better offers that served her client AND her goals, and it felt natural and organic. She had no email list and a social media following of just a few hundred people.

My client, Emma, had her first $18K month by just showing up authentically and closed clients by doing LESS sales calls, because she was finally selling the right aligned offers in a way that felt connected and REAL (not pressure based or pushy). She had a list of 1,500 people.

Another client, Jasmine, shifted her offers to be more aligned to the business she wanted to build and made $75K in sales within 2 months, and had an email list of like 300 people and a FB group of 1,000.

None of these people had huge audiences by any means. You just need to START. There are honestly clients I have who book their own clients and get sales by starting from ZERO - literally no one in their audience yet at all. They start right, follow the process we teach, show up and focus on the right activities, and then they book clients quickly. This is what happened to Mariam, who booked a client within days of joining my Academy program just following one of our training lessons.

The key you need to understand here is, you do not have to be anything special to be successful. You do not need to have come from a fancy or impressive background. You don't need to be the most brilliant person in the world. You don't even need to have an audience at all.

What matters is that you are YOU. You have your own set of skills you bring to the table, your own perspective, experience, drive, and passion. And these are the exact things that help you stand out and call in those clients faster.

You just need to start NOW and start with the right process that will help you get there. Don't doubt yourself. Don't overcomplicate your business. Don't overthink things. Just be. Just show up. You've got this.

I believe in you! Now, let's really dig in.

6

BECOMING AN ALIGNED LEADER
IN YOUR LIFE AND BUSINESS

*I*n order to have revolutionary results and turn your idea into a sustainable aligned business, you have to step into being the leader you're meant to be. It doesn't have to mean you're going after being Oprah-level famous (unless you want to). But you must step into a level of leadership in your life so you can reach the success you're capable of.

But here's the thing: You can't be a leader if you have a truckload of mindset stuff going on that's weighing you down or stopping you from showing up. So we first have to clear some of that stuff out. Because here's the truth: If you're not at a place yet where you feel visible, impactful, or successful enough in your business, 9 times out of 10 it's because of *you*.

That's right, it's not because of your environment, it's not because you don't have enough money, or because your website isn't branded beautifully enough. It's you, reading this book right now, you.

This might be making you uncomfortable right

now. You might even be getting angry, thinking "But Kamila, you don't know my story! I've tried it all, I've tried showing up, I've tried growing my audience, I've tried getting out there. It's not me. I'm just unlucky."

Or maybe you're sitting there thinking, "This Kamila chick doesn't know what it's like to grow a business when you have 5 mouths to feed, kids to dress in the morning, and then go to day job for 9 or 10 hours, before I can finally have the time to work on my business at night."

If you're thinking any of these things, I want to first of all acknowledge you: You're not alone. I've heard an iteration of the above from many students and clients over the years, most of whom were able to change their situation and rise above it to create the life they desire. And look, I get it. I don't want to discredit your experience or make you feel like what you're feeling isn't relevant or real. The world may often feel like it's not on our side. And look, all kinds of challenges happen for every single one of us. What matters most isn't that it's happening (because we can't control that) - it's how *you respond to it* that shapes your life and determines the life you'll live (and how your business will shift as a result of it).

Let's say you were working at a day job. You had a toxic boss and eventually got fired because you could just never get on the same page. It happened. How did you react? Did you fume and get angry and pout about it after? Get down on yourself, blame them, feel angry... and maybe binge drink to ease the pain as you vent to your friends - and then kept doing it day after day, for weeks? Or did you get determined to find a job that WOULD treat you right, you went right to the job search websites, updated your resumes, contacted some recruiters and went to work? Because if the boss can't see your value? Screw them, let's find someone who WILL - because you are worthy. *(Or maybe you decided, oh heck let me start a business and I can be my own boss and teach my employees way better - hehe ;-)*

Do you see how the same exact situation can be treated completely differently? One is coming from a place of victimhood and hopelessness, and the other is coming from a place of leadership, responsibility, and power.

You get to choose how you will act at any given time. And the way you choose to act and behave will inform whether you will reach your ultimate goals sooner.

There are three key things you must do in order to get out of your own way and step into confident aligned leadership that creates the income and the impact you desire. Let's go into each one next:

Key #1 - Your Worthiness Story

Remember how I talked about not feeling good enough in one of the previous chapters? Well, this conversation is really about worthiness. Do you *actually* feel worthy of having the success you desire?

I understand this is a hard question. Consciously you might be saying yes, while subconsciously your mind could be screaming HELL NO. You might not feel like you're ready. You might feel like you aren't pretty enough, skinny enough, intelligent enough, creative enough (blah blah blah) in order to create the success you want. Or maybe you're too young, too old, too serious, too busy. Whatever.

Trust me, I understand! This was the reason why I shut down the doors to my photography business in 2013. I was surrounded by the hottest of the hot in the Chicago nightlife scene, which made me feel nothing short of the least attractive person in the crowd (and this was BEFORE I gained the extra 30 pounds after starting my next business!).

Four nights per week, I watched as handsome wealthy men flirted with beautiful supermodel-looking women, as I captured the process with my camera. Four nights per week, I was on the sidelines admiring the glitz and glamour, the wild fun mixed with sex, drugs and electronic music, as I desperately wanted to be a part of. Four nights per week, I would put on my face and pretend like I belonged.

But despite living this life for 6 years... I never did actually feel like I belonged. I became so obsessed with how I looked, with that craving to fit in, I developed an eating disorder, coupled with excessive drug and alcohol use, and recklessness in adult behaviors that would make Led Zeppelin proud.

That obsession turned into self-hatred which turned into more self-destructive behaviors that eventually caused me to question what I was even doing with my life. The bottom line was that I did not feel *worthy* of belonging, I did not feel *worthy* of feeling desired and admired, I did not feel *worthy* of being happy.

Where was that coming from? After all, we all are born perfect innocent beings. We could speculate for days on the reasoning behind why we turn out the way we do. I could talk about how your upbringing and childhood plays a part in your current mindset, I could talk about how your surroundings matter, I could even talk about genetics. But there's a reason why I didn't go for a PhD in Psychology and it's because I'm not your therapist nor do I want to be.

What I do know is that through years of self-reflection and my own personal development work, I learned that our actual life is a mirror of our inner beliefs and emotions... and those emotions tend to guide our actions.

> If I feel like shit, I'm going to behave in a way that supports my feeling like shit. Getting *aligned* with feeling like that, if you will. It's a self-fulfilling prophecy.

What does this mean for you? Well it means that you are subconsciously creating your own reality every single day. We could get stuck on your backstory and blame your parents for poor judgement and lacking money management skills but let's be honest... It still brings it back to YOU. After all, if your upbringing was the *only* thing that mattered, we wouldn't be hearing about countless rags to riches success stories from entrepreneurs who go from homeless to seven figures.

So it has to do with YOU. And your relationship with yourself is centered around your own feelings of worthiness. How do you really feel about the possibility of being a successful leader and entrepreneur? When I ask this question, what comes up? Is it a feeling of certainty and excitement, or is it a "yeah right, if only" skepticism? Neither response is right nor wrong, it's just information to understand yourself better. Because the first step to getting out of your own way and onto path of leadership is self-awareness.

If you *are* feeling certainty and excitement, like there is not even a millimeter of a shred of doubt about your ability to show up and lead confidently, you're ahead of the curve and can likely skip the rest of this chapter. If, however, you're like the 99.9% of the people reading this, and there's even a slight shred of doubt about yourself and whether you are good enough to become that thriving confident aligned leader, keep reading.

THERE WAS a client I once had who was a very skilled graphic designer, let's name her Alicia. Alicia had been doing graphic design for her clients for several years, but she had started to feel like she wanted to empower her clients in a different way. She wanted to start teaching and coaching people how to use design and branding on their own to grow their own businesses. She felt like this switch would help her create more leverage in her life while increasing her income, but also helping more people on a bigger scale. The whole "teach a man to fish, feed him for a lifetime" concept, ya know?

> *This is actually a huge thing we teach our clients in my programs. Learn more here:* **http:// heartbehindhustle.com/bonustraining**

I agreed. If she wanted to coach, let's get her to coach! The problem came up, however, when it was time for Alicia to actually start offering her new services to people.

She talked to two or three prospects, all of which said "no."

Alicia felt deflated. She felt discouraged. She knew she wanted to start making a bigger impact with her gifts and talents, and knew she couldn't do it on a bigger scale if she kept doing done-for-you work. However, the few people she offered the new program to turned her down! Feelings of unworthiness crept up.

"Maybe I'm not good enough after all. What do I even know about design anyway? Why would people want to learn from *me* when there are so many other people teaching this stuff? No one wants this, I should just quit!"

Perhaps you've had feelings like this come up for yourself in the past. Here's an interesting thing: It's not like Alicia was the only person in the world who had been turned down by a prospective client. There are countless people who are getting turned down for their services each and every day. I know that might sound depressing but it's really NOT! That's the nature of business and sales. It happens. But the most important thing here is that it's not like Alicia has never been turned down before for her done-for-you work! She has! But yet hearing a NO from a prospective done-for-you client didn't trigger as strong of an emotional response as the coaching prospect did. So, what was the difference?

What you don't know yet is that Alicia was feeling uncertain about her role as a coach and teacher. She had only done this work as part of her done-for-you packages and for friends. She had never charged for her services as a coach and because of this, feelings of uncertainty were already present when she began offering the new packages. She knew she could really help people and she felt passionately about doing so, but because of her lack of *paid* experience caused her to doubt herself.

Because she felt insecure about her new offering, that feeling quickly developed into unworthiness and that, in turn, made her consider shutting down the doors to *her ENTIRE business.* The ENTIRE thing!

She started to think that her dreams of creating a scalable business were stupid, and she began doubting her ability to make money at all. What's more is that she was selectively remembering all the NO's she received from prospects and conveniently FORGOT all the yeses, positive feedback, testimonials, and gratitude she'd get from her current clients about her incredible work and services. Alicia was creating her own reality by focusing on what was NOT working because it confirmed her belief that she's not good enough to offer coaching.

Do you see how that's a problem? Do you see why thinking this way and being unaware of this thought pattern can completely derail not only your growth but the entire progress you've made thus far?

KEY #2: Taking radical responsibility

I once had a colleague, let's call her Sarah, who was seriously talented at coming up with the most crazy excuses as to why she wasn't progressing and making changes in her life.

She couldn't enroll new clients because her computer was broken. She couldn't go to the networking event because she got a flat tire. She didn't write emails to her list because she had to make dinner for her family. She couldn't do research for her new program because she wasn't "techy" enough.

Every time we spoke, Sarah seemed to be putting off important tasks and projects that could really help her business in lieu of doing something else and then using these things as an excuse as to why she wasn't progressing.

If you're like many people, you can see a little bit of yourself in Sarah. Have you ever blamed the weather for your bad mood? Have you ever been criticized by a family member and it ruined your entire day? Have you ever blamed your ex-boyfriend for why you weren't happy when you were together? Have you ever blamed the holiday season for why you gained a few extra pounds?

I know I have! It's easier to put the blame on something external and call it a day. We like being able to have a "logical" reason that's *out of our control* for why our life isn't going exactly as planned right now.

It's easier to moan about how "all men suck!" if you've had your heart broken, as if you had no active participation in the relationship that just ended. It's easy to say your email marketing software is broken because you're getting low open rates on your emails, when in reality maybe you just need to learn how to write better subject lines. And it's definitely easier to blame your lack of success on your family, your zodiac sign, your human design, whatever - when you just haven't invested and committed to getting the work done to get that business off the ground already.

We love to displace the blame so we can move on with our lives. It's easier to blame everything around you than to look in the mirror and investigate what is *really* going on. The problem with displacing the blame is that you are giving your power away. You are exclaiming to the universe that you are at the mercy of the elements and you have no ability to influence or change anything that ever happens to you and, oh poor you, life is just SO hard right now and you can't do a single thing about it.

News flash: It's time to stop feeling sorry for yourself and start doing something about it.

And look, I'm not trying to call you out to make you feel bad. I've told my fair share of "poor me" stories too and it's something that I still have to be consciously aware of and shift out of. There are still times where my friends will lovingly point out to me that I'm being a victim about something when I had no idea it was happening. I'm always grateful for being called out, because then I can change my perception and therefore begin changing my behavior and the outcomes associated with them. Now you can, too.

What I'm talking about here is the victim mentality. Having a 'victim mentality' means a person blames their circumstances in life on others around them, displacing their responsibility from them onto another person (or people). They might also blame things on other external circumstances, which they may see as being unfair, such as attaching meaning to external things and blowing things out of proportion so that they don't have to take responsibility for their actions and what happens to them. It allows these "victim mentality" people to feel like they have the "right" to complain and receive attention as others feel sorry for them and feel compelled to help because there's just *so* much drama in their life for them to handle on their own.

Let me share a quick example:

An upset teen screams at his parent after being grounded for not doing his chores for the 3rd day in a row. *"Mom! I can't believe you did that to me, you're ruining my life!"*

Classic. If we examine that statement, which I know you've either said or heard an iteration of in the past, an interesting thing comes up. First, it's obviously putting *all* of the blame on the other person. Second, it's putting excessive weight on the action of the other person and an exaggerated result for your own life (as if getting grounded had nothing to do with the actions of the kid). Third, it's a cry for attention. Poor me! Feel bad for me, I'm such a sad little bumpkin.

But it's not just antsy teenagers that play the vicim card, we all do it. And why wouldn't you? Playing the victim makes you seem more interesting to others, it gets you all the attention, and you get to displace your responsibility and throw it on someone or something else so you never have to deal with your own crap. It's like a "get out of jail free" card.

The problem with this is that you're never in control and life keeps happening to you in a way that makes you feel like you're spinning out. It's a toxic never-ending cycle: you exclaim how everything sucks, and so you attract more of that sucky-ness to you, your overall vibe gets super low, and you feel like you're at the mercy of everything and everyone around you. That's the opposite of empowerment. It's also the opposite of leadership. Not good.

The biggest thing about people who have the 'victim mentality' is that they feel like life is happening *to* them, not *for* them, and they feel like they have no ability to change anything that happens. When in reality, every single event, circumstance, and interaction is a lesson we can use to learn something new about ourselves and the world.

If you've ever thought, "If only ___ then ___" then congratulations, that's a victim thought.

If only my boyfriend took me on more dates, then our relationship would be more fulfilling. If only I was already at six figures in my business, then all of my problems would disappear. If only I lost these last 20 pounds, then I'd finally find the courage to get on camera.

These thoughts seem innocent enough but they are victim thoughts because they assume that something needs to happen in order for you to live the life you desire - *and* it claims that you have no power to change your life *today*.

Here's an example from my own life:

In early 2016, I sold all of my furniture from my studio apartment in downtown Chicago and decided to move my life to New York City. The city of lights! My dream dream city. I was elated.

Living in New York City was something I had dreamed of for years. I was convinced I'd find my soul there and that this was the place for me. I remembered visiting for the first time, my heart feeling so full!

It was March 2016 and I was on the flight from Chicago O'Hare to New York LaGuardia, armed with two suitcases, ready to move into my Upper East Side walkup studio apartment. Sitting on the plane, I was excitedly looking out the window and telling my mom, who was sitting next to me, how I couldn't believe this was finally happening!

My dream was coming true!

The first week went great as I settled into my new life. I immediately felt that electric New York energy when I stepped off the plane and I felt like I was finally coming home. Except.... That dreamy home didn't end up being as dreamy as I'd hoped.

Now, there was nothing *terribly wrong* with it per se. The apartment was okay, albeit with not very secure and pretty darn old, but at 450 square feet, it was larger than most studios in the area. The neighborhood was nice, although being 15-20 minute from the closest subway station, it made it easier to just Uber everywhere instead (which was fine since I'd rather ride in a Prius than be stuck in a poorly ventilated train car filled with body odor of sweaty strangers). And the concrete jungle vibe was okay, since I lived fairly close to Central Park, which allowed me to get my daily fix of nature.

So... you know, overall it was okay. Different from what I was used to, but okay nonetheless. Besides, my heart was filled with possibilities and knowing I had acquaintances living in the area made me even more hopeful.

But... here's what I quickly realized: An introverted entrepreneur working from home, living in a brand new place (even as cool as New York City!), where she only knows a few people, makes for a really lonely time. After a full day of work, I often felt way too tired to intentionally expose myself to the awkwardness of trying to meet new people in a bar or a Meetup.com event. It'd just take so much energy that I didn't have. I began to envy women I'd see strolling down the street with their group of girlfriends on their way to brunch. I was jealous of people's "going out" pictures on Tinder and Bumble showing how full and fun their lives were - cause OMG we live in NYC! - when my own life was filled with sitting at home watching Netflix on a Saturday night, wishing I had friends in this new city that was quickly turning into more of a drain than an energizer.

I felt really damn lonely. And I began to blame all the things around me for my loneliness. I blamed the men on dating apps who swiped right but wouldn't keep the conversation going. I blamed the acquaintances I thought I had who flaked on meeting up time and time again. I blamed the city itself for being too intense, smelly, dirty, and for overpromising and underdelivering on my expectations. But most of all, I blamed myself. I blamed my introversion for keeping me stuck where I was. I blamed my overweight body for refusing to release the pounds I gained and continuing to crave sugar every hour of every day. And I blamed my naive nature, for assuming life could get any better, when clearly you can't possibly have everything always go right in life.

I was stuck in that victim mentality spiral for an entire year without even realizing it! And trust me, those thoughts? They are vicious! They are relentless! And they will shift and form to become so convincing that you feel the truth of them in your body, along with the disappointment and anger, that just doesn't let up.

But they are *lies*. These thoughts are poisoning your mind and letting you take the easy way out. I could have continued to blame the city, the people, the energy, the cockroaches, the rats, and myself for my disappointing experience living in the city, but I decided to stop.

This way of thinking was making me bitter and resentful. And let's be honest, when's the last time you felt joy *and* resentment at the same time? Exactly. It's impossible. You're either angry or you're happy. So which will you choose?

When I moved out of my New York apartment 10 days before my lease was up, I was asking myself the same question over and over again. "What's wrong with me? How could I have failed so badly? How could I have turned my dream into such a disappointment?" I decided I must not deserve to have a dream life, as I moved back into my parents' house, sleeping in the guest room, wondering what the hell I'm supposed to do now.

I won't bore you with the rest of my story right now, but a few weeks later, I was speaking to a friend and she asked me an important question, **"But did you try?"**

Such a simple question. I was in the middle of telling her about my NYC experience, and she saw right through my bullshit. She wasn't buying it. She knew I was hiding.

"Did you try?"

The statement stopped me in my tracks. *Did I?* Did I try to make my experience better? Did I do everything I could have done to make my experience more pleasant? I blamed my acquaintances for flaking on me, but how many times did I actually reach out to them to hang out? Not many. I blamed my introversion for keeping me reserved, but did I ever challenge my comfort zone and step outside of it to seek new connections? Like, maybe twice. I blamed the city itself, but did I take advantage of being in it fully?

No, no, and no. I guess I didn't really try.

And it hit me. I was acting like a victim. I was blaming all these experiences and circumstances on everything around me, including my personality traits and qualities, so I didn't have to actually deal with the situation itself. I was unwilling to get uncomfortable, to face the music, and realize that I actually had complete control over my life. But I didn't try. So why would the universe provide if I wasn't willing to open up and receive? To step outside my comfort zone? To grow?

Exactly. This is why it's so important for you to look at your own life and notice where are you holding back right now. Where are you feeling bitter, resentful, or disappointed, and ask yourself, "But are you *trying*? Are you doing what you can to make your life become the way you DESIRE it to be?"

If you're not happy with your sales, are you putting yourself in situations where getting more sales is an option? If you feel invisible online, are you actually actively trying to show up or did you do it once and give up? If you feel like your email list isn't growing, are you sending traffic to your landing pages to get people to sign up, or are you just wanting it to grow magically on its own?

Do you think a true confident visionary *leader* would let others walk all over her? Do you think a *leader* would let life just happen to her as it may, like she's just this buoy on the water, letting the waves crash against her, unable to take the situation into her own hands? Do you really think *a leader* would give up this easily, without standing up for what she believes is right, what she deserves, and giving it her all?

Of course not. This is why playing in the victim mentality is the quickest way to step *away* from your leadership abilities and step *into* hiding. When you don't take full responsibility for your life, you can't possibly create the life you desire. Because, like, how would you even do that?

Right. So taking responsibility. Taking ownership. And showing up, uncomfortably, to look at what's not working and seeing how *you* can actually contribute to finding the solution, not seeping deeper into the problems and wishing it just wasn't happening to you.

Life doesn't happen *to* you, it happens *for* you. For you to step up, show up, and do something about it. If it was easy, everyone would be doing it.

Thankfully, now you can start investigating your life and situations and stepping up more confidently moving forward so you can become aligned with what you ACTUALLY truly desire. You're welcome. (I see you!)

Key #3: Embrace being different

Here's the thing: we all have mental stuff we deal with on a daily basis. You're not crazy, broken, or weird for having doubts, playing the victim, or being afraid of growth. We all do it.

However, most normal people don't get to see the level of success they desire, and that's because most people *are* normal... and so they live normally. They're average. They do what's expected of them. They're the norm. They don't challenge their beliefs, the status quo, and what's possible. So they settle.

The norm is that you find yourself a good day job, get married, have kids, retire when you're 65 (if you're lucky), and then survive the rest of your years living off a small amount of money each month coming in from your retirement.

Most people are completely content with this. However, there's a shadow side to this normal "steady and secure life". Did you know that when you live the norm, you have a 10% chance of getting laid off from your "steady" job EVERY YEAR? (2019, Vice News) Or if you and your partner just had a baby, they might not be able to get any paid paternity leave depending on where you live? (2020, WeForum) Or that even after you retire, you might have a 40% chance of needing to rejoin the workforce to be able to afford a basic lifestyle? (2017, RAND corporation study).

That doesn't sound very secure to me. Why would you want to live a life where your only purpose is to spend most of your life in an office, surrounded by people you can't stand, doing soul sucking work you hate? You really DO only live once. Do you want that life to be spent feeling miserable?Besides, if we're being honest... you're probably not really all that *normal* after all. Because most normal people don't feel that fire in their belly, telling them to get out there, and make an impact with their message. Most people are content staying in their "secure" corporate jobs and living for the weekend so they can finally relax and do what they *actually* enjoy doing - just two days each week.

I know you've felt that deep burning desire to make an impact and to help others. You might have known since you were little that you were meant for greatness. It's just that over the years that desire has gotten shelved away as "real responsibilities" took its place. But you know there's a huge amount of potential hidden inside of you. You can feel it!

Allow yourself to daydream a little... What would living in your potential allow you to create in your life? Perhaps you'd be speaking on big stages, writing best selling books, or working with dream clients who sing your praises. Perhaps you'd be living in your dream home, in a beautiful location, driving your favorite car, and spending so much time with your family. Or perhaps you'd be going on exotic vacations to faraway places, so deeply happy and fulfilled because your kids are getting to see their parents *living* the dream and *inspiring* them to work for what's possible for themselves and everyone around them.

Do you see it? Do you feel it?

Now if you're an avid self-help and personal development reader, you're probably expecting me to tell you that it's within reach, just keep dreaming and visualizing and it'll become your reality! Wrong.

Here's a little truth slap: it's not unusual for a person to daydream about their dream life. I mean, yes, many people don't even allow themselves to want more and dream of what's possible, BUT there are still many people who do it on a fairly regular basis. They dream of a better life, they visualize it, they wish and hope for it. So this, by itself, isn't a groundbreaking development. And most of those people? Still stay stuck. Because here's the thing: dreaming and visualizing by itself doesn't create change. What does create the change is MASSIVE aligned action.

Because most people will wish and hope and dream, without *committing* to their vision and doing the necessary work towards actually achieving that vision, creating their dream reality, and *changing* their life. They stay stuck, except now they'll also be resentful, because they know they want more and they know they *could* have more, but they aren't willing to get uncomfortable to change their reality and achieve it.

But the good news is? You've started on the action already! You've started a business that has the potential to grow if you commit to growing it properly. That's great! Just that, on its own, sets you apart from the norm. Yay!

Now that we have some of these alignment essentials out of the way, let's talk strategy.

PART II

ALIGNED MARKETING™
METHOD

7

LAUNCHING AN ALIGNED BUSINESS

*L*et's talk about your aligned business.

Obviously I don't know if you already have one created or not. The vast majority of this book will be written as if you already either have a business or at least an idea.

If you don't have a business yet, I wanted to help you out as well so you don't feel too confused.

Short version:

Our recommendation for most people who want to get started making money online is to create a service-based business, working with clients individually. While many gurus might say that e-commerce, affiliate marketing, or joining an MLM are the keys to making money online, I find that these are NOT the fastest ways to do it and they are certainly not the most impactful ways either. (More on that in just a minute)

You picked up this book because you want to make a difference in people's lives, and because of that, working with clients is the best way to do that. You don't have to worry about the crazy amount of technology that's necessary if you were to run an e-commerce store. You don't need to worry about building a gigantic audience (or running loads of paid ads) if you were to make any money as an affiliate marketer. And you don't need to slide into countless of strangers' DMs and harass your friends and family to buy your company's products if you were to start with network marketing.

Now, don't get me wrong. You can be successful with all of these, too. And there are people that run these businesses with integrity. However, from my experience they are NOT the fastest way to start making money online.

What we want you to do is identify what can you help people with. What is a problem people are experiencing right now that you have the ability to solve? What are you good at, skilled at, talented at that you could turn into a business? Is there anything you love talking about so much that people always ask you for help with? Perhaps all your time spent exploring personal development courses and reading self-help books could turn into a life coaching business. Perhaps all the time you spend creating content on TikTok could turn you into a video strategist for other businesses. Perhaps your passion for health and fitness could turn into a weight loss accountability coaching company. There are so many options!

I get into that a little bit more in the bonus video. So make sure to watch that as soon as you can, and don't worry - it might take a little while to get this one figured out. Keep reading. You don't know when clarity will come, but one thing I want you to know for sure: clarity will *not* come from you just sitting there passively thinking about stuff and not taking any action.

So what is the easiest business to start?

I can guarantee you one thing - it is not a brick and mortar store and it is not a product based business. Yes, creating a shop where customers can go in and buy your stuff can seem awesome. And it's probably what people think of when they think of a "real" business owner, but having a real "in person" business is hella expensive. First of all, you need to lease a space. Then, you need employees because you can't possibly do it all yourself, can you? Then, you gotta pay for furniture, decor, and more. That doesn't even include the products. All of that may cost five figures a month just to start. And that's before you made even a single sale! Yes, that's a real investment many "brick and mortar" business owners have to make. But what if you don't sell products? What if you sell services, like a spa or a salon. Sure. But everything still applies. You need to put a lot of dough in ahead of time to open this space up. Again, this is all before you've had even a single sale. Starting a business isn't cheap. Especially when it's done IRL. (And I don't even mention the devastating experience so many brick and mortar businesses have been dealing with during the pandemic we're experiencing in early 2020).

So brick and mortar is out. What about e-commerce? Making your own products, planners, jour-nals, candles, whatever and then selling them through an online shop or through places like Etsy. Sure. But if you're thinking of being profitable fast, it's also not the fastest or easiest business to start. In fact, most product creators and sellers barely break even. You have to pay for the materials, make the products, ship them, store all of the inventory. It all adds up in time and lots of money. So selling your own products? I don't think it's the easiest business or fastest to start.

Now, you might be wondering about dropshipping. Dropshipping is basically where you have an e-commerce store and sell products online that have already been created and manufactured overseas (usually China). How it works is you basically buy the product cheap and sell it at a profit. So, let's say you pay like $3 for a product, then you sell it for $15 or more. The manufacturer ships the product so you don't have to have any inventory at home. Sounds like a dream, right? It can be. But I personally think it's also a little bit like gambling. Everyone is selling the same exact products and it's a matter of whoever spends the most on advertising wins. And if you aren't good at ads, or your website isn't very good, or you picked the wrong product... well, tough luck. You gotta keep going. And the problem is, too, that most of these drop-shipping websites aren't building a real brand with repeat customers so it becomes a little bit like a one-trick pony. Definitely not the foundation for a long lasting legacy.

So what's left?

. . .

WHAT IS **the easiest business to start?**

In my experience, it's a service-based business.

Honestly, I try to tell my friends about this all the time but I think they discredit it because of how simple it sounds. But it's true. You sell services to people who need them. And you sell and deliver it (mostly) online. Simple. No need to overcomplicate it. That's the leverage-based way.

Now, in case you're not sure what I mean when I say "service-based business" this simply means you would be selling "help" or a "solution" to a specific person who has a challenge or problem or pain they are looking to solve. This can be as clear cut as selling social media marketing services, accounting services, design, or it can be a bit more holistic like personal finance, accountability, health coaching, spiritual coaching, or psychic readings.

The core is, you find people who are struggling with something or have a need they need to fill. That struggle or challenge has to be significant enough where they would actually pay to solve it. They also have to **be able** and **be willing** to pay for it. Then you get in front of those people and tell them you have the solution. That becomes a no-brainer offer.

So, how do you know what you should sell? I have a quick process I can take you through to help you identify your niche and focus. We're going to look at this very strategically. But before I go there, I wanted to mention alignment. Since alignment plays a big part in this whole business and marketing thing.

Whenever I go through any steps, strategies, or

suggestions in this book or my trainings, I want you to listen, take note, and then ask yourself what feels the most aligned for you to do. What does aligned mean? It means it feels right for you AND it would make sense for your audience. It would make sense for your vision, your goals, and your personality. So alignment means it's the right course of action because it makes sense, it will serve you, it will serve your people, and it feels right.

One word about this too, though, alignment doesn't always mean that things feel GOOD. This is a common misconception. In fact, usually they wouldn't feel good at all (at first) because anytime you do something new, it typically feels uncomfortable. You might feel resistance to it, your fear might pop up and try to get you to stay in your comfort zone, stay the same and not change. Just because your comfort zone and fear is telling you "stay here, don't do that" doesn't mean that the choice you are thinking about making isn't aligned. You have to access a deeper and higher part of yourself. The part that is limitless, filled with possibility, and potential - you already have it within you. Let go of the fear and scarcity thinking or limiting thinking like "But I could never do that anyway" or "I'm not the kind of person who does this" or "This would never work" or "Who am I do this anyway?" when you haven't ever tried it before. We'll talk more about this throughout the book as well.

Ok, with that little disclaimer, let's talk about the strategic 4 step process you can go through to find your niche or what you should do in your business. I also talk more about this inside the bonus training series you got as a part of this book.

4 STEP PROCESS to Finding Your Aligned Niche

How do you figure out what to sell and to whom? You can go through this process to give you some clarity in finding your niche. This is meant as a tool, not the end-all-be-all. There are many ways to find what you should be doing as a business. Sometimes it comes naturally without any strategic process at all. You see a need, and you think "I could do that!". Done. Sometimes it's providing a solution you were looking for a year or two ago as the person you were back then. Sometimes it's going off of what people are asking you for help with right now and instead of always helping people for free, it's making the decision to start monetizing it after that. So you see, usually finding the right business to start is an intuitive process and it's often based on common sense. But sometimes, we are too close to our own situation to find the right course of action. So this process, hopefully, will help. So what do you do?

First, you want to make a list of all the things you are good, skilled, talented at. Make an exhaustive list. What do you do at work? What do your friends ask you about often? What is your degree in? What have you done a lot? What do you think comes super easily to you that doesn't come quite as easily to others? What do you do with joy? Sometimes it's hard for us to come up with the things we're good at. Some people struggle with admitting they're awesome. But guess what? You are freaking awesome! So it's time to toot your own horn and admit it.

Got the list? Ok. Next step is to cross out everything you would dislike having to do all the time, and circle everything you actually enjoy doing. So, for example if you are an accountant in your day job but you absolutely freaking hate it, you feel super burnt out on it, and even if you were to do it on your own (without a job or a boss) you'd still hate it, then cross that out. On the other hand, if a lot of friends ask you about personal finance and you dislike the taxes part of accounting but you love the numbers part, coming up with savings goals, investing, and all that stuff, especially when you're doing it for people you like... And your friends seem to be shocked by how well you are able to use your salary, where they often ask you questions about it. And you enjoy doing it? That'd be one of the things you'd circle. Continue circling the things you enjoy doing from the list.

Next, you want to find out what do people actually want... and cross out anything from the circled items that doesn't match that. What is something that is actually solving a need or problem for people where they'd be willing to pay for it? For example, if you really love doing crossword puzzles, that's great. But do people want that as a service? Um, probably not. You'd cross that out. If you like personal finance and helping others with it, and you realize that yes people do want it (as in, they are asking you or other people questions about it) this is a good thing to keep. Keep going.

Next, we can remove anything that people want but are NOT willing to pay decent money for. Now, to be clear, we are focusing on *services* here, like I said earlier. People may often want to purchase things like your drawings, your books, and stuff like that. But for the purposes of this exercise, we would cross that out. So for your dreams of selling your art, you can keep it as a side project for now, let's first find a service you can sell because it will be easier and faster to make money from it, and do it more consistently, ok?

So, what are people wiling to pay for? Are people willing to pay for personal finance help? Probably. Are people willing to pay for graphic design? Sure. If you aren't sure if people are willing to pay for help in these areas, a good idea would be to do a little bit of competitive research. Go to Google. Look up these services you want to provide. Do they exist already? Are people already selling them? How much are they charging? If people are already providing these types of services, that is a GOOD thing - it means there's demand. Keep going.

Lastly, we have to find out who would be willing to pay for that, and what price point usually would make sense based on the service and based on who's buying it. For example, if I am selling personal finance coaching and accountability, what kind of person would be willing to pay for that? Well, probably someone who has a decent amount of money already right? So, the ideal person here I'd guess would be someone who's making high five or six figures per year in their salary but they still seem to still be living paycheck to paycheck and don't know how to manage that money... BUT want to learn how so they can buy a house in the future. This person would see value in spending a few hundred dollars a month in this type of service, because the return they'd get would make it worth it. A person that would probably not be a good fit is someone who is making maybe less than $50K a year, UNLESS your service was priced at a level where it made sense for them. In the future, you can also create lower priced group programs, online courses, and other products to sell as a part of your business, so you can still serve that market - just not right now. However, as you get started, my recommendation is to be clear on who can pay a premium for a service so you can sell less volume of the package but still hit your income goals.

Common question: "What if I want to help everybody? Like, anybody could benefit from my services or the thing I want to help them with?" For example, let's say you want people to get better with their fitness. Perhaps you're a

personal trainer and want to move into the online space to become a fitness coach. Great. Who can benefit from that? Yes, of course, everyone can! But targeting everyone is the surefire way to make your message resonate with no one. When you try to target everyone, your message becomes diluted, bland, and generic. Because you will then lack a bit of that specificity and that oomph that can only come when you have clarity about who you are talking to. So, yes. Even if your services can help everyone, I promise you there's a way to specify it just enough so it still feels aligned and right for you. You don't have to say "everyone" but you can say "people who already are exercising but want to get a bikini body" as an example. That's already more specific. Makes sense? Ok, moving on.

WITH THAT COMES the last element we want to consider, which is: whom from the list do you have access to right now? For example, if you identified that the best ideal person for the thing you want to sell is a high-level CEO of a Fortune 500 company, but you have none of those people in your network right now and you have no easy way to access those people to get into a conversation right now, then obviously that would not be the best approach to take when starting out, right? It's like an uphill battle, you're only going to make your job harder for yourself. So instead, you want to identify from all the people who would be willing and able to pay for your services, who can you connect with right now, the easiest, to get some of your first clients? You'll want to start there once we get into the sales part of this book. So pick the service and the people to target that are the lowest hanging fruit - you can easily get them into a conversation, they probably already want what you're selling, and you could sell it to them in a way that makes it a no-brainer for them.

Through my years of coaching entrepreneurs, I've noticed that a big mistake many beginners often make is attempting to sell services to people who don't really care to pay for them. Or selling to people who see the value in the service but just have no ability to pay for them anytime soon. For example, let's say you want to help college students with their anxiety. That's great and so important. However, thinking about the average college student, is that someone who typically is willing and able to invest in something like that? Maybe some of them, sure, but definitely not the vast majority of them. And definitely not life coaching priced at a premium. I know when I was in college, even though I had my weekend photography gig, I was still pretty damn broke and opted for free things whenever possible (plus, my school had free counseling), and preferred to spend money only on the essentials. When I needed help with my mental health, I went to therapy first and looked at getting health insurance to cover it. Now, I'm not saying life coaching isn't good for people in that age range... but we are looking at making things as easy for you as possible, right? Why would you set things up where you are more likely to struggle?

So, what if you are really passionate about college students, though? What do you do? Should you just not help them? You totally can! But you do have a business to run. So, a way you can still help people who can't or aren't willing to pay for the services you offer is by either doing them pro-bono (for free) or providing free content online (like videos, posts, emails) that people can use to get help with (this is what I do). Then, of course if they want more help, they can hire you or buy your stuff. But they should be able to get value from your free stuff too.

With that, I would still make sure you are targeting mainly ideal clients who do have the money to spend, and then you can also have *some* content directed towards the audience you are passionate about that isn't able to pay a premium. Like, if you want to help people find their dream job. Your main goal would be to help people already in careers and jobs, ideally making a decent amount of money who want to now get their next job and make it a higher-paying dream job. Then, you can ALSO dedicate, say 10-20% of your time to creating great free content for college students as well to help them get their first good job after college. Make sense? Ok good.

So naturally, you want to be tapping into your heart and alignment as you go through these exercises. What is feeling right and would be the fastest path to your vision and growth? My goal is to educate you and give you all the information you need so you can make the best, aligned, and strategic decision for you.

4 CORE MARKETS When Finding Your Niche

Another thing I wanted to talk about are the four

core markets we usually see in the services people sell online. Typically all the information and services and "help" people sell tends to fall into one of four main categories. These categories will usually thrive no matter the circumstances, because people ALWAYS want help with these four.

These four core markets are HEALTH, WEALTH, HAPPINESS, and RELATIONSHIPS. These are also four core main desires everyone wants which is why most of the highly-selling services tend to fit under at least one of these markets.

Now, there are some exceptions to this. Sometimes a service may be more of a luxury service, where it's not necessarily helping people solve a pain or challenge, it's more making something good even better. In which case, it would not squarely fit into any of these. For example, services such as interior design, teaching crocheting, learning languages, or anything else that's a hobby. These are great services and great information you can sell for sure, but they fall under more of the optional or luxury category in most cases, which means there are some different considerations to keep in mind when it comes to pricing and sales. So just be aware of that.

So within each core market, we have submarkets. These are a bit more specific topics or categories of focus within each market. Ideally, you wouldn't be focusing on just relationships as a whole in your business as that's a bit too broad. So, for example, here's how these core markets could potentially break down:

- Health —> Fitness, Nutrition, Weight Loss, Beauty
- Wealth —> Real Estate, Investing, Personal Finance, Entrepreneurship
- Happiness —> Spiritual Growth, Personal Development
- Relationships —> Dating, Parenting, Personal Growth (Relationship to Self)

And then each submarket would also go deeper into the niche and subniche. For example, the submarket is Entrepreneurship could break into niches such as Online Business, Coaching Business, Brick and Mortar, E-Commerce, etc. So your business could focus on a submarket, which would still be a little bit broad, but if you add a "flair" or "angle" to it, it becomes more specific and more niched.

For example, if you want to focus on dating, you can go a bit deeper and focus on dating for women over 40, or dating without using online dating apps, or dating after divorce, or dating to find your soul mate quickly through spirituality practices, and more. This is now your niche.

If you aren't sure what your niche would be, or maybe you are fresh out of coaching school, or you just don't know what your "angle" should be yet and how you prefer to help people, don't worry. The best way to figure that out is by working with clients. The more clients you work with in various areas, the more you will get clear on what you enjoy helping them with and what you dislike.

Make it your goal to help as many people as possible until you get a bit more clarity. But also, do note that you don't have to be perfect. I didn't get clear on my niche for years. I just showed up, helped entrepreneurs with marketing related things, and eventually after years of help, I narrowed down my approach and angle. So don't rush it. Remember, clarity comes from action - not overthinking.

My recommendation is to be just specific enough to stand out but not so specific you're making your life harder where it becomes more difficult to find people to actually work with.

3 TYPES of Service Businesses

Lastly, I wanted to get you clear on the types of service business that are out there. We probably should have talked about this sooner, but I wanted you to get some of your own thinking done first.

There are typically three categories of service based businesses:

- Done-For-You - where I do the thing you want, for you (agencies and freelancing)
- Consulting / Training - where I tell you what to do, and then you do it.
- Coaching / More Collaborative - where we do it together, you arrive at your decisions, not me, but I may guide you there. It's more collaborative.

How does this look like in various industries? Let's take the area of finance again as an example.

If you're more in the Done-For-You space, you could be like their bookkeeper or accountant. So this is basically, it's the job or the freelancing role. You are doing the thing for them. They say they need something done, you do it. Simple, straightforward, and actually a lot easier to get paid for because it's a tangible outcome they are getting. However, you become a freelancer so you make money based on how much you work, and that kind of situation can be unpredictable and way too reliant on your time, which isn't ideal in the long term - but could be a great way to get started. People are always looking for people to outsource their tasks to. As you get started, you can be the person who takes over some of these tasks for people. A great place to get started looking for some of these "gigs" are places like upwork.com.

Next, let's say if you focus on consulting. In this situation, you could be the finance advisor that helps your client make decisions. Maybe you'll come into the business, do an audit of how things are looking like and what needs to be optimized to have the business be more profitable, and then tell the entrepreneur here's a list of things you need to do to increase profitability. Or if you're a tax expert, you could lay out your tax strategy for the business so they end up saving on taxes and they can spend money on the things strategically to end up saving more on taxes using ninja tax hacks or whatever. From there, it's up to the client or their team to do the work. You may train them on how to do them, you may not. But the core is - you tell them what to do, and then they have do it.

Lastly, if you are more in the coaching space, you could be a financial coach. So this could look like you have coaching calls, the person comes to you with concerns and you work through them together but typically rather than telling the person what to do flat out, you coach them through it so the entrepreneur can potentially arrive at that conclusion themselves with your help. In traditional coaching, they say that you should not tell the person to do anything, the client is meant to arrive at every single decision. All you can do is probe and ask questions to help them make these decisions. I personally think that kind of coaching, while can be helpful in some areas, in the field of finance might not make sense. So you'd probably still have a bit of the consultant hat on, but you'd work on things together, potentially talk about some mindset stuff that comes up with money, and more. I find that a big thing that differs with consulting and coaching is that consulting is more direct and driven by the consultant, whereas coaching is more collaborative and often focuses a lot on accountability and mindset as well.

Something to consider here is that these various levels do not have to be mutually exclusive. You can have various levels of offers in your business to help people at various levels. So it's very possible you may do all three levels of support for people at various times! It really will depend based on what your people are actually wanting, what is the easiest thing to sell to them that feels aligned for you and for them. Something to keep in mind is that done-for-you often is the most pricy option, whereas coaching is the least - however this is really different based on the business: their experience, their infrastructure, and more. You will have to select the price points that make sense and start with the offer that makes the most sense as well.

Alright, let's talk more about offers in the next chapter.

8

CREATING OFFERS YOUR CLIENTS WILL LOVE

*O*ne of the most obvious first steps to actually making money online is... selling. Obviously. But, what do you sell?

If you already are established in business, you might have already identified what your approach or niche is. That's great. But if you aren't making six figures per year in your business yet, there's clearly something off that needs to be addressed. We'll do that in this chapter.

The key to making great money online (without selling your soul) is learning how to create the right offers that actually serve your clients (and you) in the most powerful way. Let's talk about the three keys to making your offers actually sell.

Thing #1: Your offer has to be congruent

One of the biggest mistakes entrepreneurs make is creating offers and then basically *forcing* the prospect to buy them: basically selling things to people who don't need them. That means, you come up with an idea of what you wanna sell, and then you try to have each person you speak with fit the mold for that particular offer and that offer only. So, you end up coming into the sales conversation with a specific expectation: This person must buy this one particular offer.

That is not good. You want to make sure, most importantly, that the offers you sell are *congruent* to the person you are selling them to. This means that you are NOT selling sand at a beach (things people don't need). Instead, you'd be selling them ice cream or maybe a beach towel. So, you want to focus on selling what people actually want and need. You have to listen to each person you speak with, and then cater your offer to them. AND if they are not a good fit for your offers, do NOT sell your offers to that person! You do not need to work with everyone. The world is an abundant place and there are more than enough people who are a good fit for your programs. If someone wants to work with you but you can't help them, do not take their money. If you do, and they have a bad experience, you have now damaged not only your trust and reputation with this person but you have done damage to the whole industry because you become yet another person who sold something they could not deliver on. Plus, it's just out of integrity. So don't do it. You can't help everyone. So focus on finding people whom you CAN help instead.

Thing #2: You want to have a variety of offers available at various price points

People will usually fall into four camps.

1. People who are hesitant to hire someone but are potentially open to it.
2. People who are sold on YOU and ready to go all in because you're amazing and they love you.
3. People who want to take this task/challenge off their plate already and willing to pay whatever it takes for someone to get it done.
4. People who see no value in investing in themselves and prefer to figure things out on their own (or, as it usually ends up being: get stuck trying).

If you are only focusing on selling ONE type of offer, you are minimizing the amount of opportunity you can have to impacting people in various situations. With that said, as you scale and grow your business, you may want to shift, specify, or limit the amount of variety in your offerings, because you will at that point know what tends to sell best and what you enjoy delivering on and what gets you the best return. However, before you have reached that six figure mark, my recommendation is to have a variety of offers available that can help people are various levels and needs.

Have a way to help someone who isn't ready to go ALL in yet (maybe it's a single session). Have a way to help someone who wants you to do it for them and be your brain basically (maybe that's a done-for-you consulting package). Have a way to help someone who wants to go alllllll in because they love you (maybe that's a long-term coaching package). An offer may look the same for each person, but often it might not. To be clear, this does not mean you should be customizing the features and the structure of your offers to each person. It means you should have a few options available for various packages (I usually recommend 3) to help people based on their needs.

This also means you have to be adaptable and present the offers to people in a way that makes sense and is the most obvious to them as the best option. We'll discuss sales in more detail later in the book.

Thing #3: You only need 5 things to sell an offer

MOST NEWER ONLINE entrepreneurs think that in order to sell their services and offerings online they have to have alllllll these things in place. They have to create a digital course, film videos, set things up in a members platform, have a sales page, automation, technology... all of these things. And guess what? You don't actually need any of it!

When I was starting out, I was under the impression that I needed all the bells and whistles, too. I didn't know any better. So I spent all this time creating a pretty website, lovely sales pages, making sure my copy was great, I had nice graphics, I filmed all these videos to share with clients... all before I had any clients at all. Then, it turned out that the first client I got was someone who knew me when I had my photography business and wanted to be mentored by me. The next person came from referral. The following came from a Facebook group. And while having a website and having these materials might have helped, they were definitely not THE things that got me these clients. What did? It was *me*. I did it.

So, you only need a few things to sell your offers. You need:

1. The name of the offer
2. The price of the offer
3. The problem and the outcome (the before & the after)
4. The delivery outline (optional)
5. The package for the offer

To go a bit more deeply into each so we are all on the same page...

The name of the offer ideally would be outcome oriented and clear. One of the biggest mistakes creative entrepreneurs make is trying to make their offer names clever rather than clear. Your audience might not know what you mean if you're using slang, inside jokes, language you use (but they might not) and just overall overly creative. One of my first coaches would always drill this phrase into me: "A confused mind does not buy." The sooner you remember this, the sooner you will have an easier time selling. So your offer name ideally would literally just say what it is.

If you are selling done-for-you services, the name of the offer does not have to be super sexy anyway. For example, I could name our agency's Facebook Ads services something fun and quirky, but why? So instead, when I talk to people on the phone, I only have two options for Facebook Ads. It's either Facebook Ads Management only, or Facebook ads management with coaching. That's it. Not sexy. But very clear. And people are buying.

If you are a coach or a consultant, or you have several levels of packages that are kind of similar but have some differences in price, or you are selling a group program or course, you will want to come up with a sexier name than just "Coaching package." A way to do this is by adding in something that will be outcome or benefit oriented.

For example, if you selling weight loss coaching for brides-to-be, you can call your coaching package, "The Fit Bride Intensive," or if it's a group program or course, it can be called "The Fit Bride Bootcamp." It's pretty clear, right? If I am a bride and I want to look good and feel fit at my wedding, then this is the program for me.

Another example, if you are a relationship coach and you are selling your coaching services to couples who want to reconnect, instead of calling your program just "relationship coaching" you can call it "Reignite the Spark: 4-Month Private Coaching Program for Couples." So there's still the clarity that it IS a coaching program, but the name is also benefit oriented. Yes, I want to reignite the spark. Bring it on!

The next thing you need to know is the price of the offer. Your price point has to be aligned with where you are in business, how much demand you currently have for your offers, how much overall experience you have, and more. If you are brand new, you aren't going to be pricing your offers very high because that'd be out of integrity for your clients, yourself, and the industry. Plus, it will be harder for you to book clients because you probably aren't emotionally or energetically aligned with that price point yet anyway.

There are a ton of high ticket coaches out there who will tell you to just double rates because you can, or to charge $25K for a program because why not? Or better yet, to "charge your worth."

Well, here's the thing: I will NOT be the person that tells you to charge $10K for a program when you aren't ready and you can't deliver 10X the value for that price point. I will also not tell you to charge your "worth" because you can't put a price tag on worth. You are worth EVERYTHING. Your self-worth and your pricing do NOT have to be connected. In fact, remember this: the SUCCESS of your business does NOT mean YOU are successful or not successful. YOU get to decide whether you are successful NOW. Yes, right NOW. The external results are just data, just insights, and just information to help your business - and **they have NOTHING to do with your value as a human.** Remember this. Our goal here is to get you aligned so the offers sell with more ease, it feels RIGHT, and the pricing is set for maximum profitability, not just charging the most you possibly can for no reason whatsoever.

You usually will want to start a bit lower in price point and then increase as demand increases. From there you will be able to find your sweet spot price point that gets you to the income goals you desire while keeping you at the number of clients you want to work with. So if you want to work with 5 clients at a time and make $5K per month, if your only offer is a private offer, then you better bring in $1K per month from each client. If you feel uncomfortable charging that right now, then you will either have to adjust your expectations with your income goals, adjust how many clients you are willing to work with at any given time, or create multiple offers so it becomes easier to hit your monetary goals. We'll discuss this later.

From there, as you grow, or if you strategically want to weed out certain people and only work with those who are more experienced or perhaps with companies, the pricing gets to increase to align with the expectations of those ideal clients AND with the level of results and service they will receive. To be clear, there is nothing wrong with charging very high ticket pricing IF IT MAKES SENSE. The problem is just picking a random big number and then going with it when the elements are not there to support that number.

Need help with this? Go this page: **http:// heartbehindhustle.com/bonustraining** *and watch* *the free bonus training to see how you can get booked solid with clients, even if you're just starting out.*

The next thing you want to have in place is the problem and outcome, something I like to call the "Before and the After."

You have to know what problems you are solving for people and what they can expect as a result. Because guess what? People don't want to just buy coaching. People don't care about how many sessions they are getting with you. They care about results, outcomes, and getting something specific and tangible done.

Get clear on what does their life look like before working with you (the Before). What are their current challenges, their pain points, their struggles? What made them reach out in the first place? And then paint a clear picture of what life can look like once these problems are solved as a result of working with you (the After)? What do they want to see happen? What results are they desiring? What tangible outcomes? Get clear on these.

Optionally, you may want to identify the curriculum for the program. This is not going to be relevant for everyone as not everyone is selling training, coaching, or consulting. Additionally, if you are brand new, you may not even know what the curriculum could look like since each client has their own challenges and problems they want to overcome. That's fine. But if you have already worked with clients and want to systemize and streamline things, creating an idea of a curriculum or delivery outcome, as in what you will cover with the client during your time together, can make it easier for you to sell the package, and make the intangible feel more tangible.

Lastly, you want to have a package for the offer so it feels juicy and yummy and all the other delicious adjectives you probably wouldn't use in a non-food related conversation. The package basically will communicate what exactly ARE they getting? What's the full package look like?

The common elements of a package are:

- Features
- Benefits
- Bonuses
- Access

Outline what are the features (what they are getting)? Are they getting 2 monthly private calls with you? For how long? Then the benefits - why should they care? Why is it important that they are getting these two calls? Add the benefit of each feature and bonus to make it relevant. Trust me when I say people would rather do LESS things than more things, we are all SUPER busy. They just want the result. So streamline it and make it as easy for your client to take action as possible. Next, bonuses. This is not always included but I think it's a great addition. A bonus is a feature that is optional but can really help and makes the value of the total package even higher. For example, I often offer Voxer Coaching with me for my private clients. It's optional, they don't have to use it, but many do because they love being able to access me anytime they want. By the way, this is also a part of the ACCESS - how can they contact me or reach me. Not every package will have access, particularly if you are selling a DIY program. Bonuses can also be access to other courses, DIY trainings, event tickets, or even physical items.

Making Offers a HECK YES

There's a lot involved when creating offers that people REALLY want to buy, and I definitely encourage you to watch some of the videos I have in my Facebook group where I talk about them. I want to share one big thing for you to remember here though:

Your offers become a HECK YES when the offer you are presenting is CONGRUENT and RELEVANT to the person you are offering it to, there is trust built, AND there's an alignment of the right time, the right price, and the right energy match.

What does this mean? We talked about this already. I hope you already promise that you will not be selling crap to people when they don't want it. I hope you promise to stay in integrity and remain ethical in your business by only working with people you know you can help. You won't manipulate or pressure people to buy things just so you can make money and they won't get anything out of it. PLEASE. Do you promise? Ok, good. Because the things you will be learning here and in my other trainings are powerful, so I want to make sure you won't use it for evil.

One of the most important keys to remember is that there has to be alignment. Truly, if the offer, you, time, or price is not aligned - it will not happen. It's a bit like magic. The right person at the right time comes across the right offer - and it becomes a total no-brainer to invest. The price being aligned does not have to mean it's low in cost or high in cost. It means that the price aligns with the outcome promised, experience provided, the brand, demand, and more. Just because something is cheap does not make it easier to sell. Often it's quite the opposite. Your prospect might have a lot of questions and feel doubtful about your offer if your promise and outcome is misaligned with the price. For example, if you are telling people you will help them make $100k but your offer only costs $10. Their BS meter will be going off. So you need to find the right aligned SWEET SPOT price to make it an easier sell.

There also has to be an element of trust built with the person you are speaking. Trust is built when the prospect is able to answer a few important questions before buying - this often happens subconsciously. I'll share those questions in the next chapter. Your marketing is usually the thing that helps them answer those questions. Sometimes you have to do it on the call as well. But overall, your entire brand experience helps people overcome these concerns.

Alright, let's talk about those questions people ask.

9

ANSWERING QUESTIONS THAT CREATE AN ALIGNED SALES EXPERIENCE

*Y*our business is based on you helping people AND getting paid well for it. Not only does it help you (you get to earn money to live a life you dream of) it helps them even more (they get to create the transformation they've been looking for). A huge part of that is the energetic exchange necessary for the commitment to work, and that happens by the client paying you. And paying you well.

However, it's important for you to realize that YOUR financial gain that comes from selling your offer is actually meant to be much LESS than the transformational result your ideal client will receive in terms of value. With that said, the client HAS to pay at a high level that is a little uncomfortable for them so that they COMMIT to the work and actually GET the full value (by having skin in the game and getting to work). Understanding this fully will help eliminate any hesitation or fear you might have around selling.

Let's say you help women with dating so they can meet high-value men and get into a loving relationship that will last a lifetime. While you can't guarantee they will find their husband within the time frame of your program, you *can* guarantee that if they actually do the work and show up fully in your program, they will get to learn, implement, and embody the strategies you teach that will help them meet and keep that amazing man. That's pretty amazing.

Now let's think about this a bit deeper. This woman who will be reaching out to you... by the time she feels ok with asking for help, she's probably tried a lot of things on her own. Humans are a prideful bunch and we often struggle with admitting to ourselves we need help, so when someone actually ends up on the phone with you, they're often pretty serious. They might have read the books, watched the videos, and gone to seminars, but they still aren't where they want to be. Enter: you. On the call, this person spills their guts to you. They share all of their deepest desires, challenges, pain points. You listen with care and heart. This person clearly wants help. They are ready for a change. YOU know you can help them and will be committed to helping them overcome their challenges with finding love. You present your offer to them. Let's say it's $5,000. The woman says yes. Amazing. You got a sale! She got a coach. But let's look deeper...

What really happened here? You made $5k. This will certainly help you. But for how long? A week? A month? Maybe it will pay your rent? Maybe for a vacation? Maybe for groceries. Great. But the truth is? That amount of money is pretty inconsequential when we look at the big picture. Especially if you have your eyes set for $100k+ years. But still, be grateful. That's fantastic. Maybe you celebrate for a week, and then you inevitably move on. But now let's think about this woman, your new client. She now gets to be supported for six months as she heals her limiting beliefs around finding love, around being worthy of dating a good man, and will learn the essential tools to finding the right man to date that will treat her right. Her life will literally NEVER be the same. She gets to find peace within herself through your work. She gets to fulfill her dream. Whether she finds that dream man within six months or not is irrelevant. You will help her learn the tools that will absolutely transform her when it comes to finding and attracting love. And that transformation? Lasts a LIFETIME. Now really think about this more. Is it worth $5k to have a lifetime transformation in the area of love? ABSOLUTELY!

Think about how much time this woman will save? She will no longer date the wrong guys, she will no longer feel unworthy of love (and therefore push the good guys away), and she will begin to love HERSELF more, which may in turn create results in even MORE areas of life. She might feel more confident and ask for that raise at her job. She might feel more sexy and experience a deeper sense of joy in her everyday life. I mean, that is just incredible.

And I know, at this point some imposter syndrome might be coming up for you. Maybe you're not confident enough yet to charge $5k. Maybe you're just getting started and charging ANYTHING is making you nervous. Maybe you've tried selling your offers and kept hearing "no" or just felt awkward in the process and don't know how it could ever be a sustainable. I get it. The goal of my programs is to help you see YOUR value and see that you get to charge whatever you desire and whatever helps YOU and YOUR client in the best way. Sometimes that's high ticket, sometimes it's lower ticket. It will depend on your level of experience, skill, demand, and more.

Ok, now you know that selling is service, and that getting a client enrollment is actually a SIGNIFI-CANTLY bigger benefit to your CLIENTS than it is to you. Now let's talk about helping people get over the edge and say YES. Regardless of what you sell and how much you charge, your ideal clients will ask themselves several questions before making their decision. This often happens subconsciously, without them realizing they're asking themselves these questions at all. However, you have to be prepared and understand that this is the process most people go through. When you are having sales conversations with prospects, you will want to address each of these questions EVEN IF the prospect doesn't actually come out and say it.

Question 1: Is this right for me?

When creating an offer, your prospect will want to know whether this offer is actually a good fit for them. A lot of people miss out sharing this detail with them directly. To help them answer this question, you have to get clear on who is your ideal client is, first and foremost. Who would benefit from your offer the most? What situation is this person in? What are their pain points and struggles? What do they really desire?

For example, my programs are usually catered specifically to online service-based entrepreneurs, so typically that's coaches, consultants, healers, service providers (such as virtual assistants, designers, tarot readers, etc), and even course creators, retreat hosts, and more. Why? It's because that's what I have the most experience and best results in. Can I help everyone? Maybe. Should I? Absolutely not.

When speaking with an ideal client, don't be shy in telling them they ARE your ideal client. It will make them feel good and they will feel more reassured about taking a decision to work with you. Reflect what you are saying to them, show them you understand, and let them know how your program can help. You will be able to create that easily when you put the **Aligned Profits method** into your business. We talk more about that in the Next Steps video.

Question 2: Can I trust you?

First of all, I'm hoping the simple answer you'd say here is yes. After all, you are a heart-centered entrepreneur who operates with integrity, right? So you wouldn't sell things to people who don't need them, right? You wouldn't also sell things to people when you know they won't get value from it, right? Good.

So your ideal client will want to know if they can

trust you. And unsurprisingly, telling them "You can trust me!" might not mean much if you and them are virtually strangers. Anyone can say that! So what do you do?

You *show* them they can trust you instead. Words are cheap. Action speaks volumes.

There are many ways that communicate that you can be trusted. The simplest way to do this is in the sales conversation itself. Truly listen to your ideal client, be there, stay present, ask questions, share relevant information and stories to help them connect with you at a deep level. Anyone can do this, even if you're brand new in business.

Another easy way to communicate that they can trust you is by truly listening to your ideal clients, messaging your offers to speak to them, and taking the time to understand who they are, where they come from, their emotional state, and so on. Then, actually sharing that with them. When someone can hear that you know the situation they're in and you explain it almost better than they can - they will automatically believe you have the solution. This is why it's so important to be present with your audience and truly and deeply listen. Not just to be able to sell better, but because it's the right thing to do.

There are many other things you can do to help gain that trust, things such as building social proof, credibility through publicity, case studies, and by sharing the right content that communicates that. We'll talk about more of these things inside the Align & Achieve method and this book.

Question 3: *Can I trust myself?*

This is a biggie. The truth is, whether someone buys or not is not usually about you. In many cases, a person might say no to your offer because they simply don't trust themselves. They don't trust they will do the work, follow through, and so on. They might also be skeptical of their own capacity for success. They might be worried they will back away when the going gets tough or when they start to see success. This is usually rooted in their fear of failure and/or fear of success.

So how can you help your prospect answer these questions? When it comes to creating your offer, you can strategically design it to incorporate an accountability and momentum piece that amplifies their sense of success and movement forward. We won't be talking about that in this book since it's more advanced, but it is something you can learn more about in **the Serve to Sell Launchpad.** You can learn more about that next step here: **http:// heartbehindhustle.com/bonustraining**

How can you make your prospect feel better about their decision to move forward and that they will actually do the work? Sometimes it's as easy as having them actually commit. Sometimes it's identifying whether they are worried about trusting themselves because they maybe tried something before that was similar and it didn't work out because they didn't put the work in either. Get clear on where this is coming from and how working with you will be different. How can the experience of enrolling in your product help them build trust in themselves?

Question 4: Is this worth the price?

This is a key question everyone is asking themselves. The truth is, you can charge whatever the heck you want. But at the end of the day, you have a successful business when people are actually buying your offers at a price point they think is worth the outcome. This is a biggie. Most entrepreneurs make the mistake of pricing their offers based on features. "What exactly am I getting? How many calls? Are the calls video or audio? How much access? How many videos?" And so on. If you are valuing your program based on this piece, you are fighting an uphill battle. Anytime a prospect can identify how much they are paying you "per hour" it becomes a battle of trading dollars for hours and you may get into a challenge of having them compare you to others in terms of price. You NEVER want to be compared based on price. What do you want to be compared on? Total value. Outcome. Results. Transformation. Because these things? You can't put a price tag on that, can you?

Can you put a price tag on finding the love of your life when you've been single or in toxic relationships for five years? Can you put a price tag on losing 100 pounds that you've been trying to lose for years? Can you put a price tag on starting a business that actually makes money for you for years to come so you never have to worry about being stuck in a day job, working for someone else, ever again? These are all invaluable results and transformations and you literally can't put a monetary number of any of it. However, each of these outcomes are valued differently in people's minds. Is this result something they are SERIOUS about getting? Is the current pain point or challenge significant enough where they are willing to pay to fix it? Have they tried many things before and they are at the end of their rope and willing to do whatever it takes? Do they feel inspired by your past results from other clients and want that same thing happen?

I've found that people who are not super committed will usually not see the value in what you're offering enough to buy at a high level. They might buy a low ticket class, maybe. But not always. This lack of commitment is often coupled with a sense of skepticism. Most often I see skepticism from people who are not fully ready to take the leap yet and/or those who are in the beginning of their journey. After all, the problem isn't significant enough yet. When someone is feeling like this, it's unlikely they will buy regardless of how great your offer is. No need to try to convince them otherwise or even give them discounts. They're just not ready.

With that said, your price has to be aligned with the value they perceive your offer has. You don't just pick a number out of thin air and call it a day. I mean, I guess you COULD do that... but that's not a very predictable or strategic thing to do. We want to find the sweet spot for the price point so that your ideal clients will feel a bit stretched in making the decision to say yes but not so that they never say yes at all. It's a sweet balance that comes with experience and time. The price you're offering also needs to feel aligned for you, too. If you feel resistant to selling something at a specific price point, it'll be hard to sell it no matter what. And your prospect will feel it and therefore might assume that this isn't quite feeling right. This goes for when your offer is both priced too low OR too high. You've gotta find the right price for you.

As a quick rule of thumb though, when pricing your programs, consider the ROI (return on investment). Will the client get a significant ROI from the experience? It doesn't have to be financial. It can be emotional, like feeling confident or peaceful in time of chaos. It can be reaching a specific goal they've been wanting to reach for ages, like breaking through a fear of public speaking and doing a speech in front of 100 people. Or it can be a life related goal, such as finding love after divorce. Is the outcome valued high in the client's eyes? Do they see that outcome as REALLY desirable or is it just kinda like ok? So they aren't thinking about "how many calls am I getting" they are thinking about "how would it feel to finally attract my soulmate". That's a whole different conversation and much easier to have the right client feel like your offer is MORE than worth the price.

Question 5: Do I need this now or can I get by without it?

This question is centered around their urgency to

reaching their goal. If your prospective client is not fully ready or committed to reaching their goals NOW, it will be a very hard sell. This is why it's so important to find out where the person really stands. Are they wanting to change their life NOW? Is that really true? Or is there anything that might feel like is holding them back from stepping into this TODAY? I don't even mean buying your offer. I mean taking the STEPS necessary to overcoming their challenge and reaching their goals or outcomes. There are steps involved with doing that, right? Are they fully ready and prepared to do that and embark on this journey? If the answer is no, it doesn't matter how great your offer is. Unless it's a super cheap little thing, they are unlikely to buy.

Now, it's possible that the answer to this question is a big YES but they are feeling scared. That's a different story. But this is why you want to identify their true desire and urgency towards reaching their goals overall, without the context of your program. If the prospect says they are wanting to reach their goals like yesterday, but then they start to come up with excuses when it comes down to buying your offer, that's something to get curious about.

Question 6: Do I really understand it?

My first long-term business coach would always drill this into me: "A confused mind does not buy."

No matter how excited you are about your offer, no matter how much time you spent on creating it, no matter how revolutionary you think it is... Your goal is to have PEOPLE enroll and go through it, right? That means, OTHER people who are not you ;-) But if they don't really GET what you're offering, how can they want to enroll? How can they feel excited about it?

This is a common challenge many thought leaders face. You are several steps ahead of your clients, so naturally you think differently. And unfortunately, this often means that the way you think and speak is not exactly always going to resonate with your ideal clients - mostly because they just aren't THERE yet. It doesn't mean you have to dumb it down, per se. I don't want you to communicate in a way that doesn't feel right. But at the same time, think about WHO is meant to take your program. What do they need to know? What is missing for them? If you were to put yourself in their shoes, would you understand what you're offering? Like, TRULY?

If you're ever unsure about whether the way you communicate your offer is unclear, just have your coach or a business friend listen to your invitation. Ask them to give you their honest feedback. And, this is important, do not get offended if they don't get it. It's not about you. It's about your ideal clients receiving the help they need. I know it can feel easy to attach our personal worth to our business. But it's not connected. Your business and your offers are NOT connected to your worth, ok? You are already worthy, deserving, amazing, and great. Now it's time for your ideal clients to see that and enroll with clarity and ease.

Once you've understood that this is often what your prospective client are going through, it will allow you to feel more empathy for them in the process as well as possibly incorporate preemptively answering some of these questions in your marketing, launches, or sales processes.

If you need help clarifying this, I'd love to help. Just see the next steps on this page here: **http:// heartbehindhustle.com/bonustraining**

Let's move on.

10

CREATING YOUR MEMORABLE MESSAGE

*H*ere's a fun fact: They never taught me how to write fancy cursive in school back in Poland. My handwriting looks pretty bad, you know this if you've ever attended any of my virtual or in-person events. It vaguely just looks like child's writing. That's fine. It's never bothered me... Until my 7th grade math class.

Math? What does math have to do with writing, you ask? Well, the teacher I had for 7th grade math just loved to write her notes on the projector. And she wrote in cursive. Heavy cursive. Like, the most cursive you can get. Sadly for me, not only could I not write in cursive, I couldn't even READ cursive. I mean, seriously - some of the letters don't even look like they're supposed to! It's not my fault we didn't write that way back in Poland!

So, anyway. I'd sit there in math class, copying her words off the screen based on shape - not understanding. I could copy the numbers fine, but for some reason she just loved to write out definitions as well. She was old school.

It's like - I could kinda understand what she was saying... I could kinda make out some of the words. But others? I was lost. I felt like I SHOULD get it, but I just wasn't.

What does that have to do with you? Well, your ideal client might also speak a certain type of language. It's a language they're used to speaking and they understand. They use certain words, they talk to themselves in a certain way, they think of their problems and challenges in a very specific way to them. They see the world in that unique way - a way that is relevant for them.

A big mistake many entrepreneurs make is not taking into consideration where that ideal client is at. You might think that you know better. So you talk about that thing they NEED to know or that they SHOULD care about. But all it does is confuse them more.

So back to the math teacher. The thing is, it COULD have been done better. She maybe realized her handwriting was hard to read, so she was also speaking the terminology out loud as she was writing it on the projector. (Unfortunately for me, I was busy copying the words and I kept missing what she was saying. Plus, I wasn't fluent in English so there was also that obstacle). Anyway, she probably thought she was being sufficiently helpful. And maybe she was - to some people. But if she REALLY wanted to help me? I would have liked to see the notes in print writing, not cursive. And if that's not an option, I would have liked her to speak it and THEN write it, rather than doing both at the same time. It also would have been helpful to be able to read about the lesson BEFORE hearing it in class, but that was not her style either. Because of that, I was just not "getting" half of the material.

You might think you know what you ideal clients needs best. But what if that person is actually more clueless than you realize?

That's messaging.

Messaging are the words you use to communicate what you do to your audience. The right messaging will make your ideal client feel like your offer was made JUST FOR THEM even though it's just your standard offer. It's rooted in listening and fully understanding your ideal client so you can speak the language they can understand.

More than that, it's about joining the conversation they are already having in their head.

Now, many entrepreneurs have used messaging for evil. They've taken what people think and say, and then morphed their crappy offer to make money and then dipped out with that cash, never to be heard from again. Some people have also done this to manipulate others into buying something they didn't actually want.

So this brings something important for us to discuss: integrity.

How To Do **Marketing With Integrity**

Being a heart-centered entrepreneur means that

you still do marketing, messaging, and sales - but in an integrity-based way. I want to make sure you under-stand that just because we're heart-centered and aligned doesn't mean that we're never asking for the sale, and it doesn't mean that we're not going to be utilizing marketing strategies. You are in business to make money, your goal is to make a profit, not just have an expensive hobby, right? BUT, there's a way to run a business with heart, and a way that feels good to everyone involved. My goal is to help you make the whole marketing process easier, so you don't EVER have to feel like you're crushing your soul in the process.

So what does being in integrity in marketing mean? Well, you get to stay heart-centered by first knowing you truly *can* help your ideal client, and not trying to get clients on board when you know that you can't actu-ally help them.

To be in integrity means you believe and know that you can help your ideal clients. You always want to make sure you are not scamming people. There are a lot of scam artists out there and people that are just trying to get you to pay them and then not really deliv-ering on their promises. You stay heart-centered and in integrity by delivering on your promises.

Next, you want to front-load the value so people can make an informed decision in whether they resonate with your style and if they want to work with you, ***and*** that they'd still feel supported even if they say no. Don't flip on someone if they say no to you, there's no need to be mean or rude. Know that the world is an abundant place and just because someone said to no or not yet, doesn't mean they can't be a client in the future, or a referral parter right now. How you react when people say no to your offers will speak volumes.

So, you want to help people because you enjoy what you're doing and people that pay you obviously get more access, speed, or customization from/to you and they get more detailed information and stuff like that. So, if somebody says no or if someone truly can't afford to work with you at that moment, they don't have to feel guilty or they don't have to feel shamed for it, and they can still feel like they can stay in your community because just being a part of your community is valuable through all of the great free content you'll be putting out there in the future to help them.

The next thing to remember is that you won't bait and switch on them. You're not going to sell them one thing and then not deliver, or deliver them something completely different. And by the way, this is very different from selling them what they *want* and delivering them what they *need*. If you're selling somebody weight loss because they want weight loss but you actually are going to teach them self-love, you still have to address weight loss in there, right? If they are really looking for diet plans and fitness and stuff like that, obviously in your sales conversation, it should come up and you might want to tell them that you won't be focusing on diet plans or fitness if that's not your angle, and tell them why your angle is better. Let the prospective client make the decision.

Next, you won't manipulate them or guilt them. No

creepy manipulation tactics, no guilting people into buying or not buying, not making them feel shamed for saying no or making a decision that doesn't necessarily agree with what you actually want to happen at this moment.

You also have to make a commitment that you won't abuse them or have them go into serious debt to invest in you. I can't tell you how many sales coaches tell their clients to hardcore pressure people during sales conversations that they're going to guilt them into joining and having them take out a second mortgage on their house, to get a loan, sell their car, whatever. And while people can certainly do those things if they really feel called to - after all, your programs are magical and transformational, so they can make the decisions to do that - but coercing them or guilting them to do it? That's another story. I've heard from so many people who were on sales conversations, they didn't want to purchase the program, and then the sales person starts to tear into them: "What's wrong you!? Are you not committed to your goals? You're gonna have a miserable life if you don't do this!" I think that is completely lacking integrity. Everyone has the ability to make their own decisions when it comes to investing in themselves, and it is not my business how they get the money to join my programs. I know that my people are smart enough to figure out whether they are able to do it or not. But I will NOT be the person to tell someone to take out a loan, get a new credit card, or go into serious debt. And yes, I teach people how to make money online. My clients have gotten amazing results -

getting into six figures, $30K months, and more. And people who are interested in working with me, know that. But I can't ever guarantee that anyone is gonna make money because it's up to the person to do the work and to show up in a way that allows for that abundance to come in. I can't control that. And for me to promise that and then say, "What's wrong with you? If you don't sign up for this, are you not committed? Don't you love yourself? Aren't you serious about your business?" I think that's so out of integrity. And if you're doing that, I highly encourage you to reconsider because I don't think it's right.

And lastly, you say no to people whom you can't help. So if you're talking to somebody on the phone and you know for a fact like this is not an ideal client, this is not someone you can help, or maybe you are just not vibing with their energy... You're not going to encourage them to sign up with you because you're just not the right person for them. You want to make sure you're really checking into these things and if you're staying true to these things you can use psychology-based strategies in marketing to help attract and generate the right clients for you, because you know that you're actually doing it for the right reasons and you are staying in integrity. You're doing it to support people, to help them make the right decision for them, and to have results towards their goals. And you're doing it by leading with heart and not just for self-interest only.

So, once you know you are committed to being in integrity, then you can motivate, empower, and

inspire your people to take a desired action with your marketing and your sales message.

So here's what you need to understand about human psychology. There are two motivations for people to do something:

1. To move away from pain.

2. To move towards pleasure.

Moving away from pain is actually a lot more of an effective motivator because it creates more urgency. If you hurt your knee, you're going to be a lot more moti-vated to do whatever you need to heal your knee - so that you're moving away from the pain of the knee versus preventative care, as in "I want to make sure I don't hurt my knee in the future." The preventative care in this situation is not going to be as motivating. It's not going to feel as urgent.

Now, that's not to say you can't offer "preventative care." You just have to be aware of, in terms of your messaging, how you're wording things.

As a caveat to this, focusing too much on messaging that moves AWAY from pain can create more of a nega-tive experience for people and may attract people who are in the victim mindset.

It sometimes may also be seen as a bit more manip-ulative in some industries. So you want to be asking yourself: What is the message? Are you helping people move away from pain or towards pleasure? For example:

- I'll help you lose weight — move away from pain

- I'll help you feel confident — move towards pleasure
- I'll help you meet your soulmate — move towards pleasure
- I'll help you stop feeling lonely — move away from pain
- Stop dating losers — move away from pain
- Attract high-quality men — move toward pleasure
- Heal your back pain — move away from pain
- Build a strong core — move toward pleasure
- Stop looking unattractive - move away from pain
- Start looking hot and sexy - move towards pleasure

As you can see in the examples above, some of the pain focused ones sound enticing whereas others sound kind of odd.

For example, helping with a physical ailment makes total sense for focusing on the pain. Whereas focusing on a current crappy situation (ie. If you're lonely or if you're dating losers) almost feels like you're calling people out which may make them feel bad about themselves. So, the same offer can be marketed or messaged in either one of those ways, and you'll have to identify which approach makes the most sense.

Quick tip: you will want to consider where your ideal client client is at in their journey to determine how much you want to talk about the pain.

For example, someone that might be in a beginning of their journey might need to hear more about moving away from pain, because they might not even understand that there's something positive out there - that there could be life filled with pleasure. So, in that situation, the way for those people to pay attention would be to talk about how they're experiencing as a challenge or a pain, and showing them that they can move away from it.

On the flip side, someone that might be a little bit more experienced might be turned off by you talking about moving away from pain because maybe they're not feeling it as much and they're already committed to their journey and they want to reach the positive results that are outside of that conversation already, so they might think they are beyond what you can offer them. In this situation, talking about moving towards pleasure would be a lot more powerful.

To give you a more concrete example: let's say that you help people with their fitness. If you're targeting people that are looking to lose weight and start exercising for the first time so they can get in shape, that's clearly helping them move away from pain (they are in a situation right now they are not happy with - being overweight - and that's the most motivating thing at that moment for them).

So messaging that could work for that person would be about losing 30 pounds, no longer feeling like you have low energy, no longer waking up in the morning with aches and pains, and no longer feeling disappointed with how you look.

But if you were talking to somebody that's a little bit more advanced, maybe they already are in pretty good shape, but they want to get ripped or super lean, maybe do a bikini competition or something. You'd be talking about moving forwards pleasure a lot more and having them see that ripped body, winning that competition, and so on. So basically, you want to be tapping into their mindset and really being aware of what's going on for them.

And also, by the way, just because someone is a beginner vs advanced doesn't mean that it's always going to look so cut and dry like I described above. It was just an example to help you see how you might want to think about this.

Also keep in mind you could combine them throughout your entire content, so you don't always have to keep everything super positive or super negative - a nice blend of things to provide context can be very helpful in helping people make decisions, too.

For example:

- I used to date losers, but then I realized I was doing things wrong. I learned a better way. I focused on myself and began to attract high-quality men instead.
- I lost 30 pounds in just 6 months effortlessly by focusing on a wellness and spiritual practice and connecting with God
- I healed my back pain by focusing on strengthening my core

You see, we addressed both angles to create a much stronger message.

I think it can be really valuable to talk about the pain. You just have to identify how much you want to talk about it. How deeply do you want to get into it? Is it the core of your messaging or is it just something that you mentioned so it's enough for them to be aware of and then you move on? You have to identify what that's gonna look like for your specific business.

Last important piece to consider here:

The thing about going deep into the pain with your messaging is that, yes, it often does help people take action, HOWEVER, sometimes those people might end up with buyer's remorse afterwards because they didn't make the decision from a place of empowerment, they made the decision from a place of fear.

I will also say that everybody's messaging and sales style is different. Some people tend to be a lot more aggressive or a lot more "in your face." And it doesn't mean that they're not heart-centered if they're doing it for the right reasons and it feels aligned for them. So, you just want to make sure that you're doing it with the right reasons.

However, in no way, shape or form is *shaming* someone for making a decision a good idea. Cause it's basically bullying someone and I don't want that to happen. I know I've been talking about this a LOT but it's really important. This is why I want to make sure you remember that you are working with real humans, with real feelings, and real lives. Treat them as such.

· · ·

MAKE Your Offers a No-Brainer with this Messaging Framework

How do you approach messaging offers to 10X your conversions when it comes to your sales? I want to introduce you to the BAB framework. This is something that I learned from one of my mentors, Derek Halpern.

The BAB framework stands for Before, After, Bridge.

Before:

First, you want to illustrate the person's current situation they are dealing with right now - the challenges, the pain points, the circumstances that are happening right now. This is also the place they do not want to be in since they're interested working with you. You want to identify what that looks like. What does their life look like before working with you?

After:

Then we go for the After. You have to paint the picture of the life they want to have, the future vision they crave and desire, and how their life will look differently after working with you.

Bridge:

The last element is the Bridge. This is where you share how your offer is the solution to bridge the gap between where they are now (before) and where they want to be (after).

Let's get into some examples.

One of my former clients, Camille, is a dating coach who specializes in helping people meet men in real life (IRL, as she calls it). The below is a BAB that could work for her business, and one I made up for the purpose of this exercise:

The **Before**: "Let me guess: you feel sick and tired of online dating. It seems like the guys you meet are either not a fit, boring, or if you like them, they just end up ghosting you. You're so wishing you didn't have to do it like this - there's gotta be a better way to meet men in today's world."

The **After**: "You feel confident, sexy and are having so much fun dating incredible high-quality men you've been meeting in-person every day. You're actually enjoying the dating process and you know your soulmate is right around the corner, if not already a part of your life."

The **Bridge**: "Through my program, we will get you ready to date, so you can become magnetically attractive to high-quality men and know exactly how and where to meet incredible men in real life with zero awkwardness. Goodbye lame apps.

Another example, let's go with website designer.

The **Before:** You want your business to grow but you hold yourself back from getting out there, because you're worried that your prospective clients won't take you seriously because your website sucks. It's making you feel like a fraud and like you're not good enough to get the clients you desire.

The **After:** You have a stunning website that makes you feel like a total rock star. You proudly share it online and you're seeing your email list and sales grow by up to 500% because of it.

The **Bridge:** Through my done-for-you website

design package, you will have a fully branded unique website done in less than four weeks.

A common question I might be getting here now is:

"But Kamila, there are all kinds of people I can help that have different starting points and end points. How can I do this then?"

This is most common for people who do private or custom work. Your solution is to get specific in the sales conversation by mirroring the prospective client. When it comes to sharing content out there to attract these prospective clients (we'll get to all of that later in the book), you can share *a few* starting points and end points in your sales pages and content versus *just one.*

Anytime you use this framework to communicate your offers to people, you will see they will pay more attention, feel clear about what you are offering, and ultimately, buy more easily. Good for you!

11

TURNING STRANGERS INTO CLIENTS

*W*e have to start by talking about the Aligned Enrollment Path, which is basically the path or journey that a person goes through before becoming a buyer.

Most people think that a sales process is as simple as:

- You get on the phone with a prospect
- You close them on the phone (or lose the sale)

And this is what most people focus on. They focus on getting better and better at the sales conversations, which is understandable. You've probably seen loads of sales experts saying how this is key... and they're not wrong. Being good at the entire sales conversation process is an essential part of having a successful business, of course. HOWEVER, this isn't where every sale is made in most situations.

Plus, what if you don't get that many sales calls on the calendar... what then? Who cares how great you are at the sales conversation if you can't get anyone to HAVE that conversation with? And what if you were really great at the sales thing in one industry (maybe you worked in corporate sales) and now you're a coach and you realize that people buy completely differently in this industry. The same tricks no longer work. Now what? If you only gauged your success on these two steps, it's too black or white. You are either crushing it or totally flopping. But the actual enrollment experience is a lot more complex than that. Hopefully, this will give you some clarity and allow you to take a big sigh of relief. Because if you're looking to create a long-lasting business, you have to stop thinking in the short-term.

JUST thinking about how many sales calls you get and how many people you close on the first call is just a fraction of the story. It's also extremely short term thinking, which is great for high-pressure sales but ABSOLUTELY detrimental for a heart-fueled business.

In fact, you don't just convert a person from being a prospect into a buyer and then that's that.

Here are the steps people would usually go through when it comes to progressing the relationship and enrollment. There's way more to the story you need to be aware of.

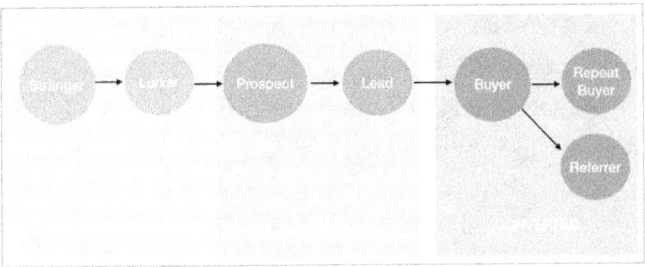

This is important because it will give you the long term view of your business and the way people progress through different phase as it relates to working with you. This allows you to maximize each opportunity and stop with the short-term thinking. It also supports you in seeing that each step you take - even if it doesn't have an immediate result - can shift your business massively in the long term.

This is extremely important especially in today's day and age. People no longer respond to high pressure, manipulative sales. While yes, some people will make the decision to buy right on the spot (I often have done this myself) there are others who need to process and think through. We'll talk more about buyer types later.

The relationship progresses through three distinct phases in the Aligned Enrollment Path, as they relate to YOUR knowledge of the person.

THE PHASES ARE:

• UNAWARE - where the person is in the Stranger and Lurker stage.

• AWARE - where the person is in the Prospect and Lead stage.

• CONVERTED - where the person is in the Buyer, Repeat Buyer, and Referrer stage.

So LET'S start with this. The first phase is the "Unaware" phase.

This is where YOU are unaware that this person, potential ideal client, even exists and they are unaware that you can really help them. They start out as a STRANGER (relationship stage 1) on the internet. They are doing their thing, browsing Facebook, scrolling Instagram....

You might have an idea of who they MIGHT be (if you've done any number of ideal client profile exercises, you can probably identify them based on their characteristics) but you don't know the EXACT person's name or contact information.

So, neither you nor them really know that something cool might happen between you two. They haven't gotten into your orbit quite yet.

But then, something awesome happens.

They get somehow introduced to you and your work! One day, as they were going through the vast universe of thousands of coaches and experts and somehow, someway, got in front of YOUR stuff.

Maybe it was your video that their friend tagged them in on Facebook, maybe they searched for something on Google and your article popped up, maybe you got interviewed on a podcast by a person they admire, or maybe someone simply told them about you so they went and checked you out.

They have now become aware of your existence. Cool! However... YOU don't really know this is happening yet. You are still totally unaware that they exist, as they are currently a LURKER (relationship stage 2)... and we all know what lurkers do. They lurk. Quietly. Behind the scenes. They're still in the "Unaware" phase, as you still don't know they're there, and they don't know quite yet that *you* can actually help *them and their unique situation.*

After some lurking and stalking, they will jump into the second phase and become a PROSPECT (relationship stage 3). The earlier Lurking phase, by the way, can take anywhere from a minute to several months or longer. The transition from the "Unaware" to the "Aware" happens when the person becomes a prospect by raising their hand and signing up for something of yours that's easily accessible that allows YOU to then identify them as a "prospect" - someone who could prospectively become a buyer. They signed up for your freebie, joined your Facebook group, liked or commented on a post, or did some other small action to make themselves seen by you. This is amazing! You now know they exist! They are curious about you, they're interested, and you get to identify them. Way to go!

From there, if they are pleased by your indoctrination into your community, your content, and the value you've been providing so far, they might transition into being a LEAD (relationship stage 4). The lead is someone who was already in your orbit and they took the next step towards possibly buying from you.

For most coaches, this is where the lead schedules a discovery call, fills out an application, or sends you an email saying they are interested in learning more about how you work.

For course creators, this is when a person signs up for an informational webinar, attends an event, or sees your sales page. They have taken that next step toward committing to the progression of the relationship and possibly buying from you. This step takes a LOT.

Most people think that people just pop out of nowhere and book a discovery call and then they book the client. They don't realize that this person they're talking to has likely gone through a LOT of stuff to get to this point. They're likely followed you for a while, or gotten a referral from someone else about you, and have been in the general mindset that was receptive to your message and work. This isn't to be taken lightly. People who ask for more help and express interest in this way are often taking a BIG step themselves, especially if you're in the personal development space. It means this person has gone from being a passive learner to taking a committed active role in their transformation. They are actually taking the steps to change their life. You and I both know how uncomfortable admitting to ourselves we need help is. This is powerful stuff!

The next phase is one you're likely familiar with, it's the "CONVERTED" phase.

Now, to get a person from being a lead and into a BUYER (relationship stage 5) - someone who has purchased from you - this is where the sales conversation takes place, whether it's a phone call, webinar, video sales letter, or sales page.

If all goes well, then the lead actively participated in the sales process and has made the decision to purchase. You have their commitment that they are totally enrolled in your vision and your program! Go you! I won't be talking very much about the different sales processes since there are a ton of ways to do that, and frankly each one would require a book on its own about it, but if we end up working together, we'll find the right option for you, no worries.

But wait - what if the person gets on the phone with you and DOESN'T buy? What happens then? Well, they are still in the LEAD stage and you will have to do more work to get them to make a decision and become a buyer. Sometimes the person will make a decision that they do NOT want to become a buyer. That's fine. Sometimes the person will decide they want to wait. That's fine, too. But in the meantime, you want to put the necessary work to show up for them and support them into stepping into the right decision. We'll talk about this more later.

So, let's say the person DID purchase and they continued down the relationship path. Think that's where it ends? Not quite! Have you ever purchased something and then had buyer's remorse the next day? Yeah, that feeling sucks. Sadly, a lot of entrepreneurs think that as soon as the sale has concluded, they are done. That couldn't be further from the truth!

Now, we want to turn this buyer into the next stage of the relationship, which is either (or both) a REFERRER and a REPEAT BUYER. This is the ultimate way to have the person show you that they are truly a believer, enrolled, and fully committed into you and your movement. These people will help you truly build your business with way less effort, traffic, or money expenditure.

Most entrepreneurs are spending 95% of their time on the transition from the LEAD and to the BUYER. But the thing is? That's not the only place where the enrollment is made. You have to enroll people to WANT to become a prospect, and then a lead, and then a buyer.

Sure, during a sales conversation you can shine with your ninja sales skills, overcoming objections, all that stuff... But if that person never actually *ends up getting* on the phone with you? Well, who are you gonna close then? Right. Or what if they end up coming onto the phone call with their arms crossed and wanting to be "convinced" because you used some weird sleazy thing to get them there before they were ready? Bleh. That's the ultimate energy drain, forreal.

The work you do before AND after is crucial to making your business flow way smoother and being a lot more profitable. I have had clients who have been with me for 2-3 years or more and spent $50K+ with me. It's because I have done my job to really deliver, nurture, and exceed expectations when it comes to the support and training they receive as it relates to where they want to be in business.

You can do the same.

12

THREE-PRONGED APPROACH TO GETTING CLIENTS

*N*ow it's time for us to talk about the full Aligned Enrollment Framework. This is the process I've outlined that pretty much ALL six and seven figure entrepreneurs use, but rarely talk about.

Why the secrecy? Well, because it's not quite as sexy as your flashy shiny objects. We won't talk too deeply about the shiny tactics, hooks, or flashy strategies this book would be a billion pages long if I even attempted to include all of them. Instead, we'll talk about the bigger strategy - the bigger picture. That's really what you need to thrive anyway. Instead of sharing bandaid solutions that might work only right now but not in a few weeks or months, I'll tell you the overarching strategy that will last through the test of time. You'll finally understand how and why this work.

And from there, if you need help with the specifics and the exact strategy for your business... well, this is the work you get to do with a strategist or coach, so take this to yours and ask them work to create a plan that makes sense for your vision. I've worked with dozens of clients and helped them enroll five and six figures in sales in two or three months without ads for their launches, and we usually would use a combination of these three prongs. The exact steps, though, are a little different for each person, so it's essential you look at your own business and identify how you can best satisfy each prong to have it make sense for your business and the results you want to achieve.

If you're ready to get help and your own customized approach to growing, just watch the free training on **http://heartbehindhustle.com/bonustraining**.

Alright, here's the framework:

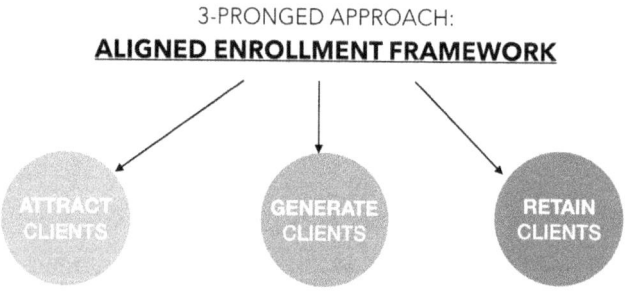

There are three prongs in the framework:
• Attracting
• Generating
• Retaining

.   .   .

LET'S start with the one prong that you might be most intrigued by if you're in the coaching space. You've probably seen people talk a lot about "attracting" clients and customers, right? How does that work?

ATTRACTING Clients

Attracting, manifesting, "calling in" clients. Such seductive words. Who doesn't want that?

Just imagine... You wake up in the morning with inbox filled with people who are just begging to work with you, and all you have to do is send them your PayPal link and boom, your bank account effortlessly grows. You feel abundant and powerful and confident. Oh, what a great life.

People talk a lot about attracting clients. You'll see most online gurus share that all you have to do is call them in and that this is THE ONLY way to grow sustainably.

The thing is? This is just ONE of the three approaches to creating enrollment and if you ONLY rely on this one thing - you will end up overworked and underpaid.

But wait, what does it even mean to be ATTRACTING clients?

As I said earlier, "ATTRACT" is the first prong of the Aligned Enrollment Framework. This is where you "manifest" your clients (if you're woo-woo), or if you're a marketing person, you use "inbound" strategies to bring these fabulous people in. This is energetically also the "feminine" energy approach to marketing as it is based on the "pull" energy of receiving (But don't worry - it doesn't mean it has to be used by women only, in fact, gender identity has nothing to do with it - we all have feminine and masculine energies regardless of what gender we associate with).

If you're like, woah. "I still don't know what you're saying, lady!" I totally get you! So let's talk about that.

How does this tangibly look like?

Well, usually this is where a prospect reaches out to YOU to inquire about working together. They're coming to YOU, hence "inbound."

The problem, particularly in the coaching or personal development space, is that when you hear that you can "attract" clients, you might think you can just kick back and do nothing for these clients to show up. That's not quite right. To get these people to reach out to you and for you to "attract" them, you have to have the process or system to get yourself IN FRONT OF THEM consistently and effectively, so that they are then intrigued enough to ask about the next steps.

It feels great when this happens and works in full force. It truly does feel like flow and being in abundance. This happens because most of the time the "Attract" approach is based on organic marketing and referrals. You don't have to spend a lot of money to make it happen (unless you're doing more advanced strategies) - it's mostly a time versus money investment (but obviously often can be both if leveraged to scale).

There are so many coaches and experts I've supported who have created fantastically effective launches and gotten booked out with clients just from pure content creation and visibility on Facebook. Many of them have their own Facebook group they've grown and nurtured. Others have built an engaged email list where they share valuable content on a consistent basis. Yet others have done it big through Youtube or Instagram.

Whatever the medium, they've put a significant amount of time and effort into getting visible and known on an organic platform (even if they had some advertising dollars or partners to help them build it), and then when it came to money - they had people reaching out to them because their content was positioned well, they added value to their prospects' lives for free, and they had the numbers to support their reaching goals.

So now you might want to know which activities may specifically fall under the realm of attracting clients. These are all the things that are often seen as positioning or branding plays. Sometimes they are things that don't produce loads of results right away, and they do require an investment of time and visibility into it. Here are some examples:

- Consistent strategic visibility on social media
- Strategic live streaming with valuable content
- Video creation to be shared on searchable platforms
- Podcasting and interviewing the right people to get in front of the right audiences

- Getting referrals
- Writing blog articles and getting found through SEO or virality
- Nurturing through facebook group or email list
- Publicity by showing up in front of other people's audiences, like on other people's podcasts, doing expert trainings, guest posting, virtual summits, and the like.
- And others

So you see there's quite a bit of work you need to do to show up in front of your ideal people so they WANT to reach out to you. They don't just fall out of the sky. And it's dangerous because this is what a lot of coaches will teach you. That all you have to do is align yourself, believe in yourself, and the clients will come. They will appear out of thin air. But that's not quite the full story.

While yes, your mindset and your beliefs and your perspective WILL support these prospects in reaching out - after all every piece of content has an element of your energy behind it (so confident and attractive mindset and energy will bring in the right ideal people to you), but you still have to do the work to physically get in front of these people. Just because you're doing ten pages of journaling each morning, doesn't mean you will magically have an inbox filled with prospects if you don't change your daily habits and behavior as it relates to visibility, organic marketing, and referral generation. Make sense?

Now, most coaches will also tell you this is THE

ONLY thing you need to do. But that isn't the full story either. Focusing on JUST THIS one approach and not the others will leave you a lot of money on the table. Remember, there are THREE areas you'd want to have working in tune to truly maximize your results. You'll then have to find the right mix of each for your own unique Aligned Enrollment Framework.

But alright, let's dig into the next prong - Generating clients. This is one of my favorite things because most people either don't do it at all OR they do it totally wrong and therefore get burned. When I work with clients to help them during their launches, they often will bring in as much as 50% extra revenue during a launch JUST by focusing on GENERATING clients as well as attracting clients. I'm excited for you to discover this too.

Generating Clients

On the other side of the coin of attracting clients, we've got generating clients. These, in the marketing world, are also seen as the traditional "Outbound" strategies, or energetically this is the "masculine" energy approach to marketing, that is more proactive, "get after it" and a bit more hustle based, but also extremely effective.

In fact, the "push" energy doesn't have to mean that you are pushing people to do something, it simply means that you are the one taking charge, you are the one doing the connections, and you are just a lot more proactive in your approach versus waiting for people to reach out to you. So rather than the focus on "receiving" the focus is on "making it happen."

In tactical terms, the act of generating clients is often seen by using activities such as:

- Reaching out to people directly - cold email/warm email/DMs
- Running paid advertising, especially going directly to an offer or funnel
- Doing webinars/lives/etc with a direct pitch
- Posts with a direct pitch
- Emails with an offer

A lot of times generating clients makes heart-centered people very uncomfortable because they think they have to be sleazy in the process. And it's no surprise, there are a ton of people who will cold message us on social media pitching their services. And while that also can work, it is not the most aligned approach as it is too random, the people you'd be messaging usually would have no clue who you are, and more. So how can you ensure you are generating clients without being gross about it?

Simple - you don't prioritize reaching out to "cold" people, aka do not pitch people who have no idea who you are. The difference between a message that is welcomed and a message that is not just ignored but potentially even marked as spam is the warmth of the person who is receiving it. By warmth, I don't mean their personality or character. I mean, how warm they are in terms of knowing who you are. So, if the person receiving the message is brand new to you, you have never interacted before, and you are coming out to them with a pitch right away rather than to build a relationship - guess what? That has a high probability of being seen as sleazy and self-serving. On the other hand, if you reached out to people who were okay with you reaching out to them, for example people who request to be your friend on Facebook, people you've interacted with before in a Facebook group, people who join your Facebook group, people who follow you on Instagram, people who ask for help with something and you can help them... those people are way more likely to see your message as a welcome break from what they've been doing. In fact, I often get responses to my messages such as "thank you SO much for reaching out" and "I'm so happy to hear that you care!" - and the only difference was that I reached out to people who were at least somewhat connected to me already.

Another key thing to remember to avoid being seen as sleazy, is to send any "mass messages" without looking at who you are messaging first. You know, the ones where you write out a whole long message and then copy and paste it to a whole bunch of people. I constantly hear about people who get cold pitched products they don't care about in the DMs by strangers. I'll even get messages such as "Wanna meet your dream man?," or "Wanna learn how to start an online business?" Or "Wanna learn how to get comfortable on camera?" When taking one quick glance on my profile would tell you that I am 1) already in a relationship, 2) already a successful business owner and in fact, I teach people this exact same thing, and 3) that I go on livestream and make videos all the time. You get it. Not only will messaging irrelevant stuff to people be seen as spammy, it can also damage your reputation. Don't do it. If you plan to message someone brand new, at least PLEASE make the message very relevant to them, don't copy and paste a mass message, and offer them value before pitching.

Retaining Clients

The last element of getting clients is actually not about getting new people to say yes to you, but it's about having *current* or *past* clients say yes to you... again! In fact, renewing or reselling to clients is one of the best ways to create more cashflow in your business. These people have already put their trust in you and if you did a good job, you can get them more access and value to help them with the next level, whatever that may look like for them.

There's a known fact in the marketing world that says it costs 10x more to enroll a new client or customer than it does to enroll a past or current one. As you can see, it is significantly easier to sell to someone who's already given you money - any amount of money - for your work than it is to get someone brand new to give you money for the first time. The reason this is true is because as soon as someone takes out their wallet, their psychology changes. They are no longer thinking like a passive reader, or a lurker... they have decided that they like you and trust you enough to create a monetary transaction with you. That speaks volumes! When your offer is right, the price point works, and the value offered is relevant and desirable, it all plays together to work in your benefit.

From there, you want to make sure you don't just keep moving on to bring NEW people in all the time, you also want to make sure you are doing a great job for your current clients and getting them value so they want to keep investing with you.

There are two things you can usually do with a client:

- Renew: when you enroll someone who just ended their contract with you for the same offer, basically to "re-up" their agreement.
- Resell: when you sell your client another offer as the next step, this is usually for people whom you worked with before and you took a break or ended your contract, and now you want to get them into a new program.

The key to retaining clients is to ensure you have a strategic flow from one offer to the next. Instead of offering just one thing and helping people with just one thing, make sure to think about what the NEXT thing your clients may need help with, and whether you can help them with that. You will want to create a no-brainer next step for clients to continue working with you. The core of this is to make sure you don't just fix one problem, you are able to create an opening to go even deeper.

For example, a client may come to me wanting me to help them set up and launch their business so they can start getting clients more consistently online. They are successful and they were able to get to $3K per month. The next step is to keep growing. I can help them go from $3K to $10K a month. Great. What about after? Well they'll want to scale. So, you see - I have programs and packages that can help them at various stages of their growth - even if it's just private coaching so it can be super customized. So for future, you will want to be thinking about that natural offer and results progression as well.

The more you think about how to create the perfect blend of the three elements from the framework to work together, the more simple and easy your sales are going to come in. You've gotta put the work in to generate clients, this is a priority. But then, also make sure that you are creating content to get some of those people to convert easier so you can also attract those clients into your business. And lastly, make sure you are also keeping in mind current and past clients so you can retain them.

13

MY FOOLPROOF SYSTEM TO SHOWING UP & GROWING YOUR BUSINESS CONSISTENTLY

*O*ne of the biggest questions I get is around the "how" of growing your business. What should you do every day? Every week? And onwards?

There are a thousand different tactics and tools you can use to market your business online, so it can feel really confusing to pick which ones to listen to and which ones to discard. In this chapter, I'm going to share with you the 10,000 foot view of one of the methodologies I teach my clients that gets them to start being consistent and repeatable in terms of their marketing activities, so they never have to feel like they're throwing spaghetti at the wall hoping it sticks. Let's get started.

I have a pretty systematic mind. I like to know what steps I need to take and in which order to be successful. Once I nail that, I can veer out on my own and experiment. But I always love following the steps first. So, I want to break down the steps. We'll also talk about how to build this all together to create your twelve-month sales and marketing plan in the next chapter.

So, the Aligned Marketing Method™ is comprised of these four layers that are focused on what to do on a daily, weekly, monthly, and quarterly basis. I like to see it as a triangle.

Layer 1: Daily Profit & Visibility Activities

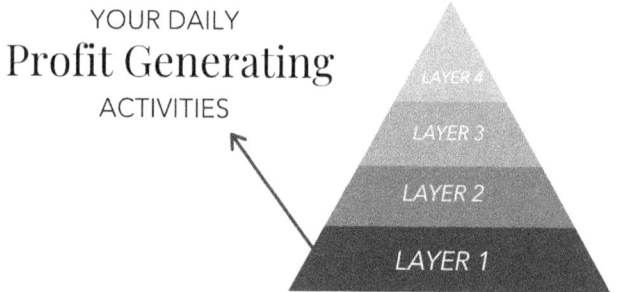

We always want to start out with the most important and the most frequently focused on activities - your daily activities. I call these daily profit generating activities since that's what you'll want to be doing most of the time if your current goal is to make money. If you want to make money, you focus on things that will help you make money. What are these things?

- Starting conversations with your audience in the DM
- Having connection calls or sales calls

- Selling in the DM (to people who are interested)
- Reaching out to prospects who filled out applications or forms
- Following up with leads or prospects
- And others

So, technically these aren't really as much marketing as they are sales activities. But the goal is for you to take action and build relationships and connections with others. After all, it's humans that will be signing up for your programs and offers, so you need to focus on making those connections with humans on a daily basis or as close to as possible.

This is actually an advantage you get when you have a smaller audience, you can manage talking to more people a lot easier and you can be fully present with those people more, which often leads to a higher conversion.

If you struggle with sales or need help having converting conversions that lead to clients, watch the video on our next steps page and let's talk about how we can help you in one of our programs: **http://heartbehindhustle.com/bonustraining**

If you're new in business, you might also be scratching your head, like "But what I don't have anyone to contact? Should I be contacting strangers?" Ideally not total strangers, no. We are not fans of total cold DM strategies, since they rarely feel good for everyone involved. We recommend building up your audience and getting in front of people and then starting relevant connected conversations instead. We highly advise you against sending the usual "mass DM" promo messages. That's the best way to get ignored.

So what do you do? Well, a part of your daily activities should also be to get in front of new people. This is how it works. You'd identify who your ideal clients are and where they are currently hanging out online. Where do they spend time? Who do they follow already? Which Facebook groups do they belong to? Which discussion forums do they read?

Then, you put yourself there in their path so that they start to notice you. When they go to your profile, it should be optimized to convert them or follow you at the very least.

"Optimized"? I realized I might be getting ahead of yourself. If you're using Instagram, you want to make sure at first glance that your Instagram is clear about who you are and what you do for whom. Utilize your bio effectively by stating your mission statement as well as next steps. Include some story highlights where you share some value. And your content should include some valuable videos, pictures, and text to help the prospect see you as someone they want to learn from.

To be clear, you don't have to be using Instagram to make this process work. Our clients use whatever social media platform they want - Instagram, Facebook, LinkedIn. It works across the board because rather than being focused on the technical pieces of the platform, we focus on human connection and how humans work and operate.

Layer 2: Weekly Content Activities

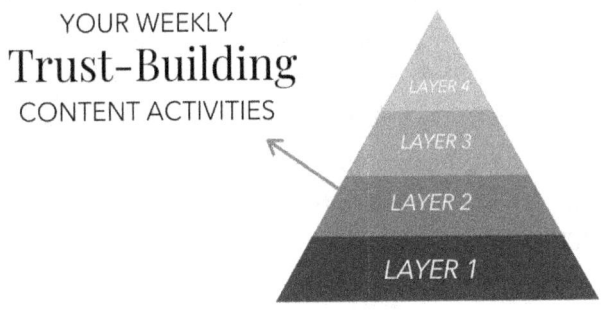

At least once a week, you should be creating an epic piece of content. Notice, I said epic not boring, usual, or generic. This means that this piece of content should be something you actually feel proud of and that provides a lot of value to your ideal clients.

There's a difference between entrepreneurs who are successful online and those who aren't, even though both might be posting all the time.

Those who struggle with growing their audience are usually not putting a lot of thought or effort into their content. But let me explain further, because this is not about how much time you spend on creating it, or how pretty your pictures are. In fact, those things matter much less than you think. It's about the content itself. What are you saying? What is your message? What is the purpose? What's the value? And is it the same thing people have been hearing forever, or are you actually providing a new unique perspective on things? Are you regurgitating the same old or are you sharing new philosophies and angles on things to help people?

This is not about posting those boring inspirational word images on Instagram with a one word caption, like "Make today count!". Who cares? To stand out in today's world, you have to STAND OUT. Make being on your account mean something. Make it engaging and like people can't get enough.

There are a few goals your content should have, and each piece of content should pick one goal:

- Goal 1. Get a lurker to become a lead
- Goal 2. Get a lead to reach out or buy
- Goal 3. Get a lurker OR a lead to become obsessed and tell all their friends about you

Most people focus on just goal one or two. Which is fine, and yes you do need to include content that does these things, too. But the thing that will make you stand out? Is having content that's created at least once a week that accomplishes goal 3 as well. This means you need to make your content BINGEABLE!

That's right. We live in a binge society. Before I began writing this chapter, I watched 3 hours of The Mindy Project reruns on Hulu. I'm not ashamed. I love to binge watch my favorite TV shows. And same for new creators I find. Once I find someone whom I really resonate with, I wanna consume ALL their content - or as much as I can in one sitting.

So what kind of content is bingeable? It's content that provides a new take on an idea, a unique perspective, and insight. It may also be a storytelling piece that helps me feel a certain way WHILE also providing value and an insight. It might also be something to help me learn a tactical piece of information in the easiest way possible. Or something else. Basically, you'll have to get clear on what you believe in, what your signature process is, and what your philosophy ideologies are in regards to what you help clients with. And then share them.

What format should this content be in? Anything works, honestly. Most commonly, our clients would start a weekly live show in their Facebook group or on their Instagram, where they go live every week - same day and time - and talk about a certain topic. Others might do this on YouTube instead. Others might have a podcast. Then others might do this on a blog and write it out, or just write it out on Instagram directly. And then someone else might do a weekly Instagram Story series.

So really - it doesn't have to be super long (but it's nice if it is a LITTLE long so it keeps the person there with you, the longer they're hanging out with you, the more they'll feel connected), but it does have to be valuable and help them with something.

This isn't the ONLY content you should ever create, but if you can start incorporating this into your weekly or biweekly strategy, you will start seeing a lot more people raising their hands and engaging with you - making your DAILY activities that much easier to execute.

Layer 3: Monthly Event Activities

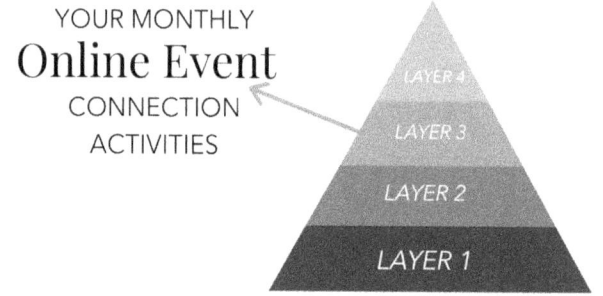

At least once a month, you'll want to do some kind of a conversion event. This really varies on the person a LOT here. Some of my clients would just take their weekly live show they do and once a month, they'd convert that into a more closed-door event for people where they share value and then also invite into the next step. You can do a direct invitation to join your course or program, to apply for a call with you to discuss a program or coaching or your services, or have people buy a session with you directly as well. Sometimes, you might not have anything to sell in which case you can either skip this activity or just do it for value only.

These events are usually happening in a way that is more behind the scenes and closed door, which means people have to register to attend. In most cases, you'd create a landing page and collect email addresses from attendees, but you can also just have them register through a Zoom link just as easily. The details will really depend on the purpose of the event as well as what you'll be doing at the end of it.

Either way, here are some things my clients have done on a monthly basis or a bimonthly basis to not only build massive rapport and trust, but also convert some of their audience into buyers:

- Free masterclass or workshop
- Paid masterclass or workshop (usually a lower ticket price to make it a no-brainer offer, but in some situations it can be mid-priced as well - depends on your overall strategy)
- Free group coaching call
- Free intuitive coaching or reading session for the group
- A cacao ceremony
- A group reiki and meditation session
- And others

The truth is, the more creative and unique you can get, the better, so that you can make your monthly event not only high converting but also exciting for you and your ideal clients. When you plan this event, you should feel pumped! You should be thinking about it, planning it, talking about it, and having people be there with you at the same level of excitement.

I also want to stress that this is not usually the typical "webinar" that you'd be doing here, although you CAN do a masterclass style of an event that is teaching based with a pitch. A traditional webinar people are used to are usually filled with fluff, way too much back story, and just an unbalanced level of value to pitch ratio, which makes the whole experience feel a little bit icky to most. You can flip this by doing a masterclass format where you DO actually share insights, you skip the whole "hero's journey" part where you talk about yourself for 15 minutes (honestly, people don't really care about you- they just want you to get to the good part!), and share the insights or mindset shifts, followed by the pitch. The experience should feel HIGHLY valuable to the right person.

We teach our aligned masterclass framework and other ways to run these events inside our programs. We can discuss whether this is a good fit for you here: **http://heartbehindhustle.com/bonustraining**

"But, Kamila! I'm afraid to pitch my offer. Won't I sound weird?" This is common concern here. I want to clear up the fact that this does NOT have to be a webinar style call. Some people just do a softer invitation at the end. They share their before and after for working together and then invite people to drop a comment in the chat if they'd like to talk on the phone. Then they reach out to each person individually with the link to book the call (exercising your daily profit activities here). Others will be more direct and won't want to contact everyone individually, and therefore they will share more about the call you can have together and then they will drop the link for people to book the call directly. Others might be more protective over the time, so they will drop an application link instead to make sure they only book a time with those who are most qualified. Sometimes you'd share the price of your offer, sometimes you won't (especially if you're offering private work and there might be multiple options available).

The more important thing to remember here is that you aren't doing a typical "pitch," it's *an invitation.* It doesn't have to feel weird and awkward. It's a heart-felt invitation to go deeper, to connect more, to take that next step. There's no need to get into what modules you get, and how much each module is priced at, and all the details when it might not be make sense for you in the context of your event.

So breathe. You can't mess this up.

Layer 4: Quarterly Launches

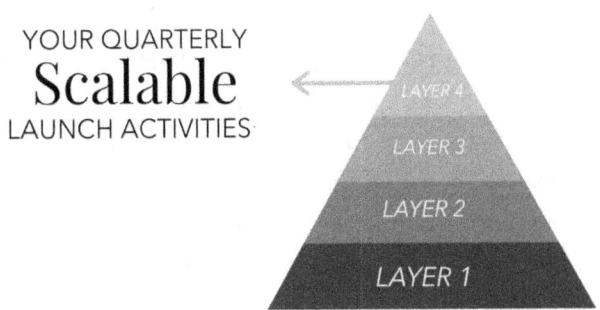

This last layer is usually more for my clients who have been in business for a little while. In most cases, they've already scaled from just working with private 1-on-1 clients and into group programs and courses. When this happens, to create a boost of enrollment, we recommend doing a launch at least once a quarter.

Launches are an extremely effective way to book clients for your scalable programs by taking prospects through a few days of valuable content, and then inviting them into a special limited-time offer.

I wanted to also mention that you can also do a launch for a private program as well! This is especially if you have several spots open for coaching, healing, or services.

We have a whole section dedicated to launching in our Academy program, and the key here is that practice makes better. The goal is to create a method or process that works FOR you so you can repeat it over and over again, whether it's every quarter to enroll into the same program, or twice a year, or so depending on your yearly plan. Why reinvent the wheel when you have something that works? We'll talk about that in the next chapter.

In most cases, when planning a launch, you don't just randomly create a launch event and then try to sell. There are stages you follow. The entire launch is actually meant to feel like an experience - it should be fun, valuable, and exciting. Not a snooze fest and not just fluff information. To stand out, you must share some of your best stuff.

Overview of Launch Models

There are many ways to launch, I want to go over briefly the most common and effective ways to do it.

MODEL #1: 5 Day Challenge.

This is the most common model, and one I use most frequently as well. What you do is you come up with a 5-day training that you deliver to people. This can be a challenge where people do something but it can be any training to help people change their belief patterns about the topic you help them with. The usual structure is as follows:

- Day 1: Introduction & Overcome initial mindset beliefs that might prevent people from taking the next step (enrolling in your program)
- Day 2 & 3: Content
- Day 4: Mix of content + invitation to your program
- Day 5: Mix of content + invitation to your program

Then you can do additional few days of either content, additional Q&As, or more. Depending on what price is the thing you're selling, you may also include fast action bonuses that disappear at various points, like a "live only" bonus that disappears after the end of live session on day 4, a fast action bonus for the first 48 hours, and then other bonuses until the doors close completely on either Monday, Tuesday, or Wednesday.

MODEL #2: 3-Day Course Recording.

This is a model where you bring people behind the scenes with you as you record a course live. This isn't something you'd be doing all the time, as you might not have courses you need to record all the time. Although in some cases, you might just run and record the same course every time you run this campaign. The premise is that you are getting people signed up to watch you record a $497 or $997 (or more!) course LIVE. They HAVE to be there live, they are not able to get a recording for free. Then you invite people to either buy the entire course at a discounted rate, or to apply for your next level program or coaching and get the entire recording of the course as a bonus. Each day is about 2-3 hours of filming so it can be a bit intensive. Here's the usual structure of each day, written in hour:minute format:

- 0:00 - 0:10 Introduction
- 0:10 - 0:45 Lesson #1
- 0:45 - 1:15 Lesson #2
- 1:15 - 1:30 Invitation to Program
- 1:30 - 2:00 Lesson #3

You can obviously change it up as well if you wish, but the core here is that you are running this entire thing, usually on Zoom, you are recording it FOR

YOURSELF not for the other people. You really emphasize that there will be no recording for them so they have to attend live.

I don't see a ton of people doing this model, I learned about it from a friend who tried it and was quite successful with it - plus she had a ton of fun and it generated a ton of buzz. I tried it a few times and enjoyed it as well, the only problem is that it does take a lot of time each day so if your not high on energy, it could be a little tough. You have to know yourself best.

MODEL #3: **Deep Dive Workshop.**

This is the other model I do most frequently, which is a deep dive workshop. This is basically taking what you'd teach in a 5 day challenge format and teach it in one 2-3 hour workshop. In most cases, I charge a small fee to attend this workshop as well. My sweet spot price is usually between $17 and $47, as my goal is to get as many people to attend as possible so I can get a decent conversion rate from attendees to applying for the next step program.

The good thing about doing a workshop like this and charging for access is that it significantly increases the live attendance. However, obviously you need to make sure you are able to run the workshop with enough people first to make it worth it. You'd ideally get at least 20 people registered, ideally 100+. So if you are new, and your current audience is really small, this might not be as easy and therefore it might make more sense to do a free workshop instead (or just do a free 5 challenge).

There isn't really a structure for this workshop that I always follow. Sometimes I'll prepare and share slides, but honestly I really hate making slides so most of the time it's just me on camera with a big whiteboard or a big post-it board. I really like that style because it also feels more intimate and like we're there together, almost as if we're there together in person. This is going to depend on your teaching style, whether you prefer having a lot of notes to refer to or if you're better off the cuff. I am WAY better with just a few written notes and going off the cuff, so I prefer to skip the slideshows most of the time.

Getting people to pay attention to your launch

Your launch is meant to bring in some serious sales, and it's not to be taken lightly. The goal is to get people to register to attend separately from just hanging out in your social media as followers or being passively on your email list. You usually would be promoting your launch event as an EVENT and giving it between one to three weeks to promote and get people registered.

Getting registrations is important because it ensures people are actually aware that you're doing this event, they know what to expect, they can put it into their calendars, they can feel like they're a part of an actual experience.

Most of the time, when it's your first launch, I recommend focusing on getting organic leads to start.

This way, you don't have to feel as stressed about the performance of the launch because you don't have any money riding on it. Promote your event on social media, amp up your daily profit generating activities, and bring in the invitation to register into your content more. Remember that most people who are following you will NOT know you are doing a launch even if you are posting about it all the time. I like to say that just at the time when you feel like you're probably being "annoying" with how much you're talking about the launch, you're finally starting to actually get *seen*.

Personally, I no longer rely on organic as much as I used to as I prefer to utilize paid advertising to run my launches, so I can save time. This is something you can do, too, if you have some budget set aside for advertising. If you're doing a launch for the first time, I recommend not spending a ton of money on ads yet. It's better to run the launch once and then get some numbers and data, so you know what to expect next time. What was the cost per lead? How many people registered? How many people applied for a call? How many ended up enrolling for your program? What was the ROI? Once you have this data, you can then amp it up and scale the next time without the need to guess.

An easy way to identify how much to spend on an ad campaign like this is - how much is one client worth? If all you got is one client, how much would they pay you? If it's $1,000 then you can spend $1,000 on ads. If it's $5,000, but they may pay on an installment plan, you can either go for the full $5k if you're feeling particularly adventurous or you can put in whatever the first month's pay would be. In most cases, starting out with $1K is a good number to start. Spending less than $500 might not get you enough people to sign up which might create results that won't be as representative of the actual launch. Try to get at least 300 people for a free challenge if you can, but if your leads are more expensive, just keep that in mind.

Alright, let's map everything out into a yearlong plan so you can see how all of these pieces can play together.

14

YOUR 12-MONTH MARKETING PLAN

*H*ow much money do you want your business to bring in during the next 12 months? What's the first number that pops up for you? Not the number that you think is SAFE... that ACTUAL number that popped up in your head. What is it?

Now, what's the emotion that came up when you thought it? Was it excitement? Fear? Anxiety? Curiosity? That feeling of "But how!?" Were you tempted to change your answer?

Now ask yourself, what do I need in order to reach this goal? A nanny for your kids? To reorganize your schedule to create more time? Joining a program to learn the strategic step-by-step so you don't waste your time figuring it out? A coach to ask questions anytime you want? A virtual assistant to take the load off? Or something else?

I like to get clear on where we're going first, as well as acknowledging that there are certain things you have complete control over right NOW to help you reach those goals with more ease. Many people set goals without any thought. I want you to be different. The truth is that you have everything in your power to change your current situation and it's already begun here. Now, I want to help you outline the next steps.

So, from the number you came up with. Do you know where that money is coming from? And it's ok if you don't. Sometimes some of the money comes from unexpected places, and that's great. We always want to leave room for unexpected magic, because when you're fully aligned with a goal income, the money just tends to show up even if you don't fully expect it to. However, I am a strategist, and as your strategist right now, we do want to have at least somewhat of an idea of where that money COULD come from.

In most cases, I like to have at least 3 offers to plan for. If you're new, this might be just your private offers. Let's say you have a private coaching container that's $3k and you also have a VIP Day option for $1k. If your goal is to reach $65k in the next 12 months, if you only focus on selling these offers, you will have to book, let's say, 15 clients at $3k (totaling $45K) and 20 VIP Days (totaling $20k). That's a total of 35 clients in the next twelve months. That's not so bad!

Now, what if you have been doing this for a little while and you have more offers in the mix.

Let's say your private coaching is $5k but you only want to bring in three clients per quarter. There are four quarters, so 3 x 4 = 12 clients total (making it $60K). Then you have a group coaching program you created that's $2K. You want to run it twice in a year because it's a six month program, and in each cohort you'd like to have 15 people. That's 15 x $2k = $30k. Do it twice, and you've got $60K. That, combined with the private coaching offer, is already $120k for the year.

Do you see how you can start mapping things out like this to see what's possible and where it COULD come from? Now I know things don't always go as planned. You might end up creating additional offers or workshops (like we talked about in the quarterly activities in the previous chapter). You might end up enrolling more or less people during your launches. You might create an in-person event, do an affiliate partnership, or something else. So the numbers change all the time. But we want you to have an idea of where this COULD come from, so you can have at least something to refer back to.

Once you have an idea of what your offers may be, you can start to map things into a calendar so you know what to focus on during each quarter. As you already know, I like to do a quarterly launch for my big program, the Academy. Sometimes I'd do it more often than that, though. The truth is, I map out my year, but then I REALLY focus on the business one quarter at a time. So whatever I map out for the next 12 months is with the expectation that it may change. Got it? Ok.

Let's map this out:

January	February	March
		Launch
April	May	June
		Launch
July	August	September
		Launch
October	November	December
		Launch

This is obviously just an example, and you could do the launch at any point it doesn't have to be the months I listed out. But from here, you can see what the focus is on overall. Now to bring it to you, what are you selling during each launch? If you want to run the same group coaching program twice a year only because it's a six month program, you will want to map that in. And then decide what to launch during the other quarters. Maybe it's a smaller course? Or maybe it's a focus to enroll into your private coaching? Or maybe it's nothing. Maybe you don't want to launch anything - say, in the last quarter you just want to chill and hang out. You get to choose based on your goals, assets available, and structure of your business.

If you need help mapping which offers to create and how to create your own unique strategy to launching them, I highly recommend watching the next steps video and booking a call with us to see how we can help you: **http:// heartbehindhustle.com/bonustraining**

From there, you want to pick the focus for the other months. If you follow our method, you know that once a month there is also a conversion event happening where you can enroll people into something else. Are you just enrolling into your private coaching? Maybe you want to sell some VIP days? Or maybe you want to do a paid workshop? You get to choose and map that in here too.

Here's an example:

January	February	March
Sell a new years workshop	Waitlist for group program	**Group Program Launch**
April	May	June
Sell a paid workshop	*Nothing*	**Launch a Private Coaching Package**
July	August	September
Nothing	Waitlist for group program	**Group Program Launch**
October	November	December
Sell a paid workshop	Black Friday sale	**Launch a VIP Day Package**

Notice how I made May and July months where you don't sell anything. That's ok to do! Maybe you want to take it easy those months and your monthly event will be just focused on engaging your audience and nurturing them instead. That's totally a-ok, especially if you're on the path to or exceeding your goals. That's the beautiful thing, too. You get to customize your journey

AND when you're doing well, you can take some time off and enjoy the ride!

I really love mapping things out this way because then I can start to really see what is the actual FOCUS this month? What am I doing? What should be the call-to-action in my posts? When should I start reaching out to people? When do I want to make sure I am really paying attention and being present, because maybe I'm gearing up to do a launch, and when can I just relax and take a vacation or something? Since you are only focusing on selling one main thing per month, it's also way less overwhelming.

I want to also make a note here and mention that you may absolutely end up selling other things during these months too! What we're mapping out here is what you focus on selling PUBLICLY. What does your marketing revolve around? However, you will end up getting calls with prospects (when you follow the daily activities) and some of them will want to join your private coaching EVEN IF you're not actively focused on selling that during that month. I hope this makes sense. This is meant to be just a marketing calendar for public sales, but there should be a LOT more going on behind-the-scenes. That's the whole thing about our Aligned Marketing Method. You'll be booking clients left and right, without necessarily having to be super LOUD about it all the time.

In fact, you might even have a calendar that looks closer to this:

January	February	March
Nothing	Waitlist for group program	**Group Program Launch**
April	May	June
Sell a paid workshop	*Nothing*	**Launch a Private Coaching Package**
July	August	September
Nothing	Waitlist for group program	**Group Program Launch**
October	November	December
Nothing	Black Friday sale	*Nothing*

... because you might be crushing it so much with your daily activities and booking clients that way. The more you show up, grow and nurture your audience, and scale - the easier your marketing calendar will end up feeling.

So then, the goal is to break down each month's focus into weekly activities. If your goal for the month is to do nothing, then obviously you can just post spontaneously and continue doing your daily activities. But if your goal is to sell, let's say, a VIP Day? You weekly schedule should reflect that.

Let's break that down a bit further, here's what a month might look like (this is a total made up example by the way):

	Monday	Tuesday	Wednesday	Thursday	Friday	Saturday	Sunday
Week 1	Post: Testimonial		promote live show	**Live Show**	Promote replay of live show		
Week 2		Post: Story about value of quick coaching	promote live show	**Live Show** (topic you might cover in a future VIP day)	Promote replay of live show	Post: Sneak peek of upcoming masterclass	Early open doors to masterclass RSVP
Week 3	*promote masterclass*	*promote masterclass*	*promote masterclass*	**Masterclass** to sell VIP Days	Promote replay of masterclass	Post: Why VIP days are great	Post: Testimonial
Week 4		Post: How to apply for VIP days	promote live show	**Live Show** (still invite into VIP Days)	Promote replay of live show	Post: VIP day applications closing	

You might end up doing more or less, it really depends on your audience, how engaged they are, and so on. Everything in your business should be seen as a living breathing thing that may change. That's why it's so important to be adaptable, but have a goal and system in mind so you have something to go along with either way.

So now, you are able to map out your year and take action on creating your plan. Remember, don't over-think it, don't overplan it, show up and do the work and you'll be able to adjust as needed.

PART III

ACCELERATING YOUR RESULTS

15

CRAFTING YOUR VISION FOR SUCCESS

*W*hen I asked my client, Beverly, what kind of success she envisioned for herself, she told me she wanted to get sales everyday in her business. She wanted to feel like every day, she woke up with email payment notifications from successful purchases from either new customers or recurring clients. Two months later, this became her reality.

When I asked my client, Jasmine, what she wanted her day to look like, she told me she wanted to work with zero one-on-one coaching clients and wanted to focus on training and group coaching since she felt way more excited about that. After a few months, she had no more 1:1 clients and was focusing on her group program full-time which had generated $75k in just 2 months during our work together.

When I asked my client, Kate, how she wanted her business grow, she said she wanted to get pregnant in a few months and she knew she couldn't handle working with as many private clients as she did. So we adjusted her business structure, added a mastermind and a membership, and she was able to cut down her hours from working 80 hours a week to 20 hours a week, while bringing in six figures a year.

And when I asked my client, Lea, how she wanted to see her next level as, she said she wanted to turn her passion into consistent clients. She wanted to stop blogging just for fun and she wanted to actually help women every day as they healed, so she could feel like she was fulfilling her purpose. A few months later, she had booked 7 clients for her program bringing her income to $3k/mo after being at only about $300/mo for *years*.

NOW THE QUESTION comes to you....

What do YOU want your business to look like as your next level? Is it to get a booked solid private client practice? Is it to scale away from private clients and into groups? Is it to start getting sales every day? Is it to start speaking on stages? Or maybe it's something else?

You want to start spending time each day envisioning what the looks like for you, otherwise it'll be really hard to reach a goal that isn't clear. And the truth is, each business operates differently depending on what you want it to look like in an ideal world. We have to keep in mind who you are, what your goals are, where you are in business right now, and more.

When it comes to thinking about your future vision and how you'd like your business to be, say 2 or 5 years down the line... There are four different roads you may want to take.

Understanding the Aligned Archetypes

Through working with so many different entrepreneurs over the years, I've been able to identify that there are usually four very different visions people have, who may all have a similar looking business to an untrained eye. It comes down to how you'd like the future to look like. What would you like to do on a day to day basis. What is important to you. As I share with you each of these archetypes, ask yourself which resonate with you the most. Where would you like to see yourself in a few years? What would be your ideal situation?

ARCHETYPE #1: **Celebrity Famous**

The vision for this person is to be known by the masses, or as I like to call it "Oprah level famous." While you might not literally be just as famous as Oprah, the goal is to step into being known by all kinds of people, including outside of your niche or industry. People here often start within a niche, build an audience then, and then start branching out and being more "mass appeal." These people have a vision of being on camera, doing a lot of press, being friends with other well-known people. They love the glitz and glamour. They want to just show up and get paid for it. Many traditional influencers have a vision of being celebrity famous as well, they just want their content and lifestyle to be the thing to get customers and grow their brand. They don't necessarily share anything that's groundbreaking in their information, many times the content they share is either aspirational, lifestyle oriented, or more beginner-friendly so that the masses can understand (but not always).

These people also may still be working with clients privately but to be completely honest, they are not too thrilled about that, UNLESS their clients are super high paying or celebrity clients. So, they might be making most of their money through either brand deals, books, and possibly low ticket products and courses. Some people who could be seen as Celebrity Famous in the online entrepreneur space are Marie Forleo and Amanda Frances.

ARCHETYPE #2: Thought Leading

This person also wants to be known, but they don't really care about being recognized or known by the masses. They'd rather be very respected and known within their industry. As such, they know that if they keep their information beginner-oriented, it won't get them far - plus talking about the basics really bores them.

A Thought Leading archetype has a thirst for knowledge and they are a visionary and kind of an experimenter in a way, as well. They are constantly pushing the envelope and developing new theories, new philosophies, and new ways of moving their industry forward. They thrive by doing speeches on their developments, possibly having a podcast, writing books.

On the surface, it's pretty similar to the archetype above. The difference here is what drives them and the level of depth they share. They have no interest in being known by everyone and their content tends to be more complex and advanced. Their books aren't books you'd gift a random person, because that random person would probably get bored. Whereas a Celebrity Famous' book, you could gift to anyone and they'd get value out of it.

This person would thrive working with high level clients either as a CEO of an agency or intimately with experienced clients, possibly leading retreats, doing speaking engagements and more. An example of a Thought Leading entrepreneur in the online space is someone like Seth Godin.

ARCHETYPE #3: Intimately Connected

This person has no desire to be famous or in the spotlight. They want to stay in the trenches by doing the work they do with their clients. Their clients are the reasons why they are doing this work, they absolutely love seeing them get results, creating a transformation, they love that intimate experience of helping someone. Frequently photographers, designers, coaches, healers love to stay intimately connected, even if they scale to $500K+ per year, they know they must have a close connection to their clients regardless. For them, that's literally the thing that drives them.

And yes, the stuff they share is still valuable. They might have their own ideas and philosophies but they are not driven to be known for them necessarily. They develop these methodologies for their clients. They also don't mind talking about the beginner stuff, as long as it helps their clients and students, they're ok with it. So it's like, they show up online to get the clients rather than just to show up because they love being in the spotlight.

That doesn't mean they don't like being on camera. They just prioritize their focus on developing their skills and getting better and better at their craft. They might not even care about having a huge company, if we're being totally honest. They want to be successful while being connected to each person they serve. The way for them to scale, as demand increases, would be therefore to just increase the rates and potentially start creating retreats, events, and group coaching programs that still have a certain level of access.

These are often the "hidden gems" in the online space. Some examples of entrepreneurs like this are people such as Pat Flynn (who isn't really *that* hidden of a gem anymore, but his care for his students trumps it all).

ARCHETYPE #4: Brand Forward

Lastly, this entrepreneur actually desires to be the CEO and be the person behind the business. They don't really want to be known for being THE person, although they might have some publicity, they really want to be the mastermind being the business, the CEO, and have the brand speak for itself. Pretty much all product-based businesses are brand forward as they focus on the product to be the main draw, not the creator of the product. The same goes for SaaS (Software-as-a-Service) companies, as well as *some* agencies.

Their goal is to build their business up to eventually run without them so they can either stay as the CEO or to sell it. They value building a solid team to run the company.

A common example of this would a company like ClickFunnels, which does have a well-known leader, BUT Clickfunnels on its own does stand on its own two feet as well. Another example was Bossbabe, before it was acquired by the current owner.

YOU MIGHT ALSO END up being a hybrid of these. There are a few specific hybrid archetypes that also exist. I won't be sharing that with you today so as not to confuse you, but I will send you an email about them soon with a video - make sure you're subscribed to our emails. If not, just contact us and we'll make sure to get you added.

Think about your vision, where you want to go. The steps you take at various points will determine where you end up. So think about it wisely as you step onto your growth journey.

16

BECOMING THE CLEAR CHOICE
FOR YOUR IDEAL CLIENTS

*L*et's start with a truth bomb:

In order to be seen as the clear choice for your ideal clients, you must first believe that yourself.

So here's what we're going to look at in this lesson: First, we're going to look at your perception and confidence. Because if you don't believe that people should work with you, then why would they? If you believe that you are not good enough to make money online, or that you aren't ready, whatever - your heart won't be fully open to receiving these amazing clients. Your energy will be closed off and you will subconsciously push them away.

Mindset is a huge topic and I'll be upfront and let you know that we're not going to get super, super, extremely deep into the worthiness and the mindset stuff in here, because, while I do it often with clients, this would require its own book. But we are going to do some work to help you feel more confident and certain about what you have to offer.

Second, we're going to look at your competitors in the market, so that you can see whether your current positioning needs to be shifted a little bit to make it easier for you stand out even more or even better.

And last, we're going to look at being the clear choice. So we'll look at how to get ahead of people's objections to alternative solutions so you can trust that you are the best choice. And by the way, this will get you some messaging and content ideas too.

Alrighty, so... you want people to invest in your services, right?

If you want people to invest in you, you want to make sure that you are investing in yourself first. You are basically a mirror for what you see in your clients. You are what you attract. Because everything that you are doing in your business and your life, that's the energy that you're bringing into your marketing, your sales and more. If you think investing in yourself is silly... well, why would your clients think any differently? Moreover, you won't really do a good job showing up powerfully if you subconsciously think that investing in yourself is silly. So how can you expect anyone to invest in YOU? It becomes out of integrity to even sell.

The truth is, YOU are your most important asset. I can't tell you how many people I see leaving themselves last, and this is the case especially for women. A lot of women are so used to putting themselves and their needs last - everything comes before them: their kids, their spouse, their friends, errands, and responsibilities... and then, who's left at the end? Yep. She is. But the thing is! YOU are the source of everything else actually working in your life! In order for everything to work the way you want it to, YOU have to make sure that YOU are fueling your heart, soul, health, and in general - yourself - effectively. I'm a huge believer that you have to fill your own cup first, so from the overflow you can pour into others'. You support others from the overflow of goodness you're pouring into yourself because without you, there is no business. If you are leaving yourself last, you have nothing in your cup to pour into others'. So if you don't see yourself as important and worthy, why would someone else see you as such?

If you treat yourself poorly, you will attract people who treat you poorly. If you don't invest in your growth, why should they invest in theirs through your services? And if you don't believe that you're great at what you do, they won't believe that either. Imagine, getting on a phone with a coach you hired who just has this whole energy of "You're an idiot for paying me this money." Oh my goodness, that would NOT feel good, right?! And that's the energy you'd put out if you didn't believe in it first. This is so important.

You are the source, the start of everything when it comes to your business, your marketing, and your sales. And not just that - it's about everything in your life, too. Everything is going to be a mirror.

So if you truly believe in your offers, people are going to believe that your offers are great. If you don't believe in them, if you don't believe that you are worthy of getting clients or if you believe that your stuff is just meh, why would anyone else think differently? You energetically are leading people into what they need to be thinking or perceiving you as.

So, how can you invest in yourself to shift your energy so that you can be in the energy of abundance and leading energetically to have people *want* to invest in you, *want* to follow you, *want* to be a part of your community, and *want* to tell their friends about you?

Well, first and most obvious is investing financially. This typically means investing in similar services or programs that you are in the field of selling that are relevant for your situation. For example, it could be hiring a coach or joining programs to help your business grow. You want to step into financially investing in yourself so you can start showing yourself that you're going to let nothing stand in your way of success.

In fact, the very first breakthrough that many beginning entrepreneurs have when joining our programs are exactly the moment when they invest at a higher level for the first time in their life. Like, they've never invested in themselves in this way (or any way!), and for the first time, they decide to just go for it and take a leap of faith. To trust. To declare that they are worthy. To declare that their success is inevitable and so much so, they are willing to bet on it. Feel how powerful that level of commitment feels. Amazing, right? In fact, there have been so many situations where a new client would invest in one of our coaching programs or courses when they haven't ever done that before, and almost immediately they get a new client or a sale or money shows up almost by magic. It's because all of the sudden they start to think differently, they expand their realm of possibility, and the Universe delivers to support you. It's beautiful.

I remember when I invested in my first long-term coach. I was petrified. I had committed to a $10,000 yearlong program and I had never, ever invested that much before in anything. I didn't even have a car! There were so many questions that came up for me:

"Am I really worthy of investing in myself? Who am I to do this? This doesn't make sense on paper, how can I do this? I am not making enough money in my business yet, how can I make this investment? Am I crazy?"

But the truth is, it was in that exact moment that I said yes to investing (with a payment plan - let's be real, I didn't have ten grand hanging out in my bank account), that my energy completely shifted. I finally started to believe in myself and more than that, I started to take myself more seriously.

All of the sudden, this moment of saying YES to myself made me 100x more committed, more motivated, more serious about where I'm going. And you can bet your ass I showed up differently than I ever had before! I was super engaged, I asked all the questions, I consumed all the content, and I put ALL the work in! And as a result, 8 months later I had quit my day job to do my business full time, which got to be generating five figures a month. I did this because I finally had real skin in the game. And I finally truly believed in the power of investing in myself, so when I showed up on sales calls with prospective clients, I wasn't just "selling." I was sharing and energetically showing them that I full-heartedly believe that this step - investing in coaching - can make a profound shift for them too, because it did for me.

If you really believe in this industry of online services or coaching, you want to make sure you're contributing to that industry and you're actively getting some support or having a mentor or joining programs. Same with if you're a healer, if you're providing energy healing or something like that, you may want to be investing in receiving energy healing from other healers too, right? It's just like when a yoga teacher doesn't actually believe in doing yoga. Like... it doesn't make any sense. This is how you show for yourself that you are in integrity as well.

Now a quick note, if you are unable to invest financially right now because you are struggling, I understand. You don't have to invest $10K right off the bat. You can start small. There are great resources to help you start investing in yourself in various ways at various price points that you are comfortable with (but yet, ideally still feeling a bit stretched by it - so you actually have some skin in the game). For example, you bought this book! That's a great start. (and again - ***thank you!***)

Ok, let's keep going. The second way to invest in yourself is being honest with yourself about what's really going on. So, anytime that I ask you a question like, "Are you really showing up the way you need to in order to launch and grow your business?" Intuitively, you'll know if you are or you are not. An answer will appear. Or, "Are you truly committed to this? Are you playing small? Are you hiding?" You will get the answers that you need, if you truly get quiet and get totally honest with yourself. If the answers that come up are not what you want to hear, that's ok. Be honest with yourself and then do something about it.

And this is why I wanted to introduce you to journaling. This is how you're going to see exactly what's going on and how you can shift your mindset to move forward. I recommend journaling your thoughts, feelings, goals, and vision consistently so you can explore parts of yourself you've been hiding from yourself and therefore finally move forward faster. A great way to get started is by adding it to your morning routine. You can also look up various books on Amazon about journaling for growth to help you with what questions to ask yourself and more.

The third way to invest in yourself is by having a consistent self-care practice. Self-care is so important. Investing in yourself in all of the ways I had already shared is a form of self-care as well, but there are many other ways to take care of yourself. For example, indulging in things that make you really happy that have nothing to do with achieving goals, growing your business, or making money.

I share this example because it's a big part of my journey, as well. After starting my coaching business in 2014, I became work-obsessed and began to source all of my self-worth from my business. So if my business did well, I felt happy. If it didn't do so great, I felt sad. As in, my whole identify felt sad or happy, it felt as if it was completely codependent on my business. In fact, I began to lose myself in my business. When people asked what I liked to do for fun, my answer was "ummm... make money? Grow my business? I don't know?" That's not a joke. I had no hobbies, no interests outside of my business. Sure, I watched Netflix shows and hung out with friends here and there, but it was to numb myself and then get right back to talking about or thinking about business. It was constant. It ended up completely burning me out after three and a half years, because I was working nonstop and taking no time for myself - no time for hobbies, developing myself as a person, for fun. And look, it's not that having a business isn't fun - it was and still is! But there has to be a happy medium, ya know? Sourcing your worth and your entire identity from one thing outside of you creates a toxic relationship. Yes, you can have a toxic relationship with anything, not just people. But I digress.

You want to identify how are you indulging in yourself and your pleasures in life? How are you taking care of yourself? Are you meditating consistently? Are you exercising? Are you eating well? Are you finding time in your schedule to work on your personal development? Are you spending time with loved ones? Are you getting massages? Are you reading books? Whatever it looks like for you, you want to identify what you love doing and then make sure to do it consistently. It will make you a happier, more productive person.

The fourth way is to always celebrate your wins, big and small. This is one of the biggest things people forget to do. Especially as you're growing your business, creating launches, selling products and services, you're achieving your goals, or even if you're just getting started and you're taking tiny little steps to get you moving forward and towards achieving those goals, but then you're forgetting to celebrate the fact that you've done them. And if you forget to celebrate even tiny, tiny little wins, like doing your first Facebook live or sharing yet another post consistently on social media, or reaching out to a potential client, or closing a sale, or whatever that looks like for you... If you're not acknowledging yourself and celebrating those wins, honestly, it's going to be really hard to maintain a state of momentum and flow. Momentum is created when you feel like you are winning and things are moving along smoothly, they're in flow. So you want to consciously look for wins in your life every single day - even those tiny ones you'd otherwise think aren't that significant.

You want to start asking yourself: *how did I win today?* What did I do that got me moving forward towards the vision that I have, towards the business that I want to have? And then **celebrate** that. Acknowledge yourself for the work that you're putting in. Even if it's just five minutes today, acknowledge yourself for putting in the work and showing up and actually leading the way you know you need to be leading.

And lastly, it's learning to receive and accept praise, support, and help. Some people feel uncomfortable with receiving compliments and praise and accepting when other people tell them they're doing a great job. Maybe you can relate? You might be deflecting. When someone says you're great, instead of responding with a simple "Thank you," you respond uncomfortably with, "Oh no, no, YOU are the great one! Oh no, no, no, YOU are the awesome one." Instead of just taking it in and receiving the compliment and the praise that we've done a great job. Not only does this make the other person feel weird, it makes *you* feel more stuck and it's like pressing a pause on your potential feeling of momentum.

A great way to start accepting praise is to look for it in your clients and even friends by asking them for testimonials. And when people inevitably start sharing nice things about you, to you- whether in text messages, emails, posts... Start to screenshot them and put all of them in a special folder specifically created for love notes. That way you can learn to bask in this awesome praise that you're getting anytime you want (and you're going to be getting a lot more of it as the year progresses so better start getting used to it!).

Additionally, you want to begin receiving and accepting help. I can't tell you how many people really struggle with asking for help. I used to have so much trouble asking for help. Coming from an immigrant background, I thought that the only way to make my success "worth it" was to struggle for it. Plus, I did know a good amount about marketing, so admitting I needed help almost felt like admitting defeat. I felt like I should be able to get this business thing, too! I mean, come on! And even once I did hire help, I was still resistant to getting help. So much so, that with some coaches I barely reached out, I barely asked questions, I barely showed up at all.

But then I'd end up beating myself up quietly and struggling! I felt stuck. But yet, the answer was right in front of me... I had even paid for it! I just needed to be okay with it and change my perception of it in order to reach it. Thankfully, I was able to overcome these challenges and now love hiring amazing people to join my team and help me grow. It's so fun!

The sooner you realize that we're all in it together, the sooner you will get out of your own way. Being in a community like ours, having a coach you're guided by, and even having team members to take the load off of you... it really makes all the difference. There's no shame in asking for help. In fact, it's a show of strength! You step into the role of a CEO. There are no CEOs out there that can run or grow the business without a team. Even if it's just one virtual assistant, or one coach, or a mastermind you're in... You are stronger when you have support. You'll be able to finally see your blind spots, you will multiply your output, and finally find ease and flow. This way, you will get to contribute to the economy even more, and everybody can rise together, plus you're going to get to where you want to go - way, way faster.

So, all of this to say:

It doesn't matter how great your strategy is or how perfect your positioning is... If you don't believe in your own value, if you lack confidence in yourself, or you feel unworthy of success, it will be a lot more challenging to enroll clients because you'll be subconsciously sabotaging yourself in the process.

This will manifest in ways such as:

- Not promoting yourself online at the level you know you need to in order to grow.
- Not inviting prospective clients to work with you, even though they seem like they might be a great fit.. just because you're afraid that they're going to say no.
- Assuming people will say no to you or reject you because of your prices or because it's not the right time for them or whatever.
- Making the decision for other people rather than just asking them and inviting them to work with you so they can make the decision for themselves.
- Over-giving free value and never asking for the sale, and then feeling resentful they aren't getting clients.
- Finding ways to waste time with "busy" work that doesn't do anything to actually move the needle in your business.

Let's talk about making a decision for other people, because that one is especially true during the time I'm writing this, with the pandemic. My clients have been hesitating on inviting people to work with them, hesitating with creating offers because they assumed people wouldn't want them or that people can't afford it right now. Assuming that people aren't spending money right now. But look, you are not psychic. And even if you are (*wink*), you just don't know what people will or will not do... until you present it in front of them.

I've had so many situations where I had people who I thought would not buy, ending up buying and even paying in full. This happens over and over again, and it's because people **are capable of making their own decisions.** Imagine that. So yeah. Let them make their own decisions. They are smart enough. Allow them to do what they need to do in order to change their life. Don't take the opportunity away from them simply because of your own mental barriers or assumptions. It's not fair to them.

If you're wondering what happened with those clients who hesitated with creating offers and selling? Well, after overcoming these mindset beliefs, they are totally crushing it:

- My private client, Cara, enrolled four new clients at $1500 each, into her new program in literally 4 days.
- Our Academy student, Johanna, enrolled her very first high-ticket client.
- And another Academy student, Laura, got 5 intuitive reading sessions booked in a week.
- Another Academy student, Ilse, got 8 new sales during her launch happening during the pandemic. Brand new shiny students. Yay!

Anyone gets to make money when they decide to stop standing in their own way.

Next, let's address this whole over giving free value thing. Many people are doing tons of free coaching, free value, and never asking for the sale and then feeling resentful about it.

And yes, I'm a huge fan of giving free value, creating great content, and sharing valuable information for people on my social media. I think that's a really powerful way of helping position yourself in the marketplace, showing that you know what you're talking about, as well as giving the generous energy out there so that more of it can flow into you, creating that flow of abundance.

But the challenge happens when you're over-giving to the point where you're sharing things online, or even privately, for free, that you think you should be getting paid for. So it starts to breed resentment. It starts to feel like people are taking advantage of you. But the thing is, if you aren't asking for people to buy your stuff or to work with you... if you aren't creating that energetic boundary, then how can you expect them to buy your stuff at all? People typically will wait to be invited. They wait for the right time. So while you'll have to make sure you are being generous and sharing great content, you still have to tap into your own heart as well and ask yourself, "What feels right to share? What will give them value, where I can continue to feel empowered and supported, and it's leading people to the next step of joining my programs or enrolling in my services?"

And then lastly, I see so many people finding ways to waste time, with things like sitting on Instagram and just scrolling for hours... or being busy but not being productive... by staying 100% in the consumption mode but not ever in creation or implementation mode. And the worst part is? It FEELS like they are working, but since they aren't focusing on the activities that actually move the needle, they then blame their situation on external things. Saying things like, "None of the strategies worked for me. This coach just didn't work for me. This program isn't right for me. Social media doesn't work for me." But when you really get honest with yourself, you'll realize that it didn't work for you because you didn't really put in the effort, did you? You didn't really see it through. You didn't really follow all the way through in the way that you needed to because if everything worked immediately, all of us would be millionaires in five seconds. And sadly, that's not the case (I wish!).

You have to recognize that when using any new strategy or any new platform, there are stages you go through: there's experimentation, there's testing, there's actually putting yourself out there, there's reaching out to people, there's tweaking things, there's scaling, and onwards. And it takes time to master each platform. *That's normal.* This is why we focus on doing it in an authentic way that's heart-centered so that you're not feeling resentful, you have the right expectations set, and you focus on serving and showing up from a place of alignment rather than being attached to seeing an immediate result and being all fussy and mad if it's not happening quickly enough. You have to know and trust and have faith that by you committing to this process, and showing up with your heart, and being there (and caring for) your future audience, it will pay back. Sooner than you realize, but you have to make sure you are showing up and proving to them you care about them first. Remember, *trust is earned.* And your consistency of action is one way of building it. So, the more you show up and help people regardless, the more you're going to get back from them as well. That's just how it works.

Now, if you're sitting there realizing that you've been - whoops - neglecting yourself a little bit lately and maybe you are resonating with a lot of the stuff I'm sharing so far, I want you to take a deep breath... because it's okay. It's not your fault. It's just how we've been programmed to be. And this is why you're here, reading this book. Reading this will bring you back to reality and have you shift into the best way of approaching your business so you can actually grow and have it feel right. You're exactly where you need to be on your journey.

Making Competition Irrelevant

LET'S now talk about becoming the clear choice by understanding your "competition." I have "competition" in quotes here because I don't actually believe in competition in the way people think of competition. That's because, honestly, I think that there is always more than enough for everyone to go around. The way people used to think about competition, where if someone buys product from person A, they will not buy it from person B ever, it just doesn't work like that anymore. Maybe that says something about a lack of brand loyalty, but I think it's more about people's desire to be expansive.

The truth is, when you have an online business that is adaptable and growing (because you will have a variety of services and offers through the years of owning a business) you'll realize that people usually don't just work with one person and then they're done forever. They usually keep buying. People work with many coaches. They buy many courses. They buy many services. And even if they bought a service from your "competitor" doesn't mean they will never buy from you. We live in a world of abundant opportunities - always.

However, even though that's my belief, I will still be using the word "competition" and "competitors" throughout the book - meaning "friendly competition" or just meaning "other people that do what you do," simply because this is the typical phrase that people are using and everyone knows what it means. So we'll just stick with that, cool? Alright.

First, I want to share a word of caution as we start digging into competitive research. I think it's good to be aware of your competitors... to an extent. As you go through this process, I want to make sure that you don't overdo it and get swept up in **comparisonitis**, ok?

If you're like, "What is that, Kamila?!" Well, I see comparisonitis as a synonym for "compare and despair." You have comparisonitis when you find your-self thinking things, such as "*Oh my gosh, this person is so much better than me. Her website is so much nicer and*

*her products seem to be so more polished and she has so
many more testimonials... I could never catch up and be as
good as her! I might as well give up now.*" And you're
spiraling out of control. So, I want to make sure that
you only do this process for pure research purposes
only. The things you'll be finding about your competitors? It's *just information*, it's just data, nothing more. It
doesn't mean that they're more better than you, have a
better life than you, or had more luck in their life than
you. It also does not mean that you can't succeed
because they're succeeding. Okay? Remember, it's an
abundant place we live in. Everybody gets to succeed.
Everybody gets to make money in an abundant way. In
fact, I'd love for you to shift that thought and turn it
into an inspiration instead. If she can do it, SO
CAN YOU!

We often have people posting their success stories
and wins in our Academy group, and when we have
some new students, they can sometimes feel intimi-
dated or like they're behind. But the truth is? It's inspiring. Think about it. This person was also starting out
where you are now, and through their commitment and
dedication and open heart, they began seeing results!
Imagine what YOU'LL be able to create when you stay
on the path, too! *head explodes* Limitless opportunities!!!

Ok, back to competitive research. Ideally you would
only do it for a predetermined amount of time. Especially if you've fallen into the comparison trap before,
you'll want to set a specific amount of time - say, 30
minutes - and once that time is up, you move on, you

stop looking at competitors and you focus back on you. Got it? Ok. So as long as you are doing it in a "research only" type of way, it is quite valuable to know your competition because these are the brands that your ideal clients are probably considering working with, just as they're considering working with you.

So the first step is to identify five to fifteen people who do what you do. Go ahead and write them down. If you can't think of anybody right off the bat, you can ask your friends or your audience who they also follow that does something similar to what you do.

For example, if you're a relationship coach, you can ask them, "Hey guys, who are some relationship coaches that you follow besides me?"

If you don't have an audience yet, that's okay. You can also ask people individually through DMs or asking in various topic-relevant Facebook groups. Don't forget to ask your friends, too! You might be surprised that people might actually be aware of others who do what you do, even if those people you asked aren't even ideal clients.

From there, you'll do some of your own research. Type into Google what you do and see what pops up. For example, type things like "relationship coach" or "personal finance coaching" or "instagram marketing expert." Go through the results. The first few pages might not be a match since they may be more from big websites or blogs, so I want you to keep going through the pages until you start finding actual real people who provide these types of services.

You can also look up the different keywords in Facebook or Instagram and see who shows up there. Just make sure that, as you're doing this, you take note of people that seem to actually have an active presence and at least somewhat of a following. You don't need to worry about people that are not active or seem to have a website from like 1980s or they don't really have a following at all (less than 500 followers), unless your gut really tells you that you need to pay attention. For this exercise, you would look at people that have a little bit of a bigger audience, typically anything over a thousand followers is usually a good indicator, but ideally they'd have 5000+.

Step two is to identify what each of these people sell and what their positioning looks like. I want you to especially pay attention to people who are serving people in a similar way as you. For example, if you're a life coach, they are also a life coach and are serving a similar audience. If you're serving moms, they're also serving moms. You can also take note of their method, their frameworks, their signature system, but these things don't have to the the same as yours because that is the differentiating factor for you guys - so it's ok for them to be different. I also want you to take note of their branding - the vibe of their brand, their language, tone and voice, and more. This will allow you to see that even if many people are doing the same exact thing as you, perhaps there is a way for you to stand out with your branding a bit so you still are able to find some gaps in how to message and communicate your brand online.

Step three is to draw conclusions and insights from

what's going on out there, for your own offers and positioning. From this research, you will begin to see some common threads, and it will become clear whether you stand out from these alternative options. You will notice their way of messaging, their offers, what seems to be working and not for them. This way you don't have to reinvent the wheel. You will also notice whether you need to be even more specific with your positioning to stand out... Or will you just allow your branding, personality, and content do the differentiating for you.

Step four is to make adjustments to your own original positioning or messaging as necessary... and then you just move on. You're done. No need to stalk these people or even follow them. This way you get to keep your heart and energy clean of any external influences of what they are doing, plus you will make sure that you don't end up spiraling into those pesky comparison traps.

Track Your Competitors Winning Messaging

If you want to take a deeper look into your competitive research and see what kind of messaging your competitors may be using **right now**, the best approach is to look at what paid advertising campaigns they are running. You can do this by going into the Facebook ads library (facebook.com/ads/library). *note, this will only work for people who ARE actively running ads.*

Once there, all you have to do is type in their Facebook business page name and Facebook will show you the ads this competitor is actively running right now. From these ads, you can identify what messaging they're using, what images they're using, where they are sending their traffic to, what offers, and more. You won't always know if theirs ads are actually effective, but you can typically determine their effectiveness based on whether they've been running for a little while and how much engagement the ads seem to have. For example, if an ad you are seeing has a lot of engagement, they've probably been running it for a while - and it's probably working quite well, right? Otherwise they probably wouldn't be running the ad. This is a goldmine to see what your competitors are spending money on, so you can see what types of offers are currently working.

When using this tool, it's possible that you will not see any ads running. If you don't see any results, it's because your competitor page does not have any ads that are currently actively running. This will be common if you selected smaller pages as competitors rather than those with many thousands of followers (who typically have more of a budget for advertising at that stage versus newer, or smaller pages).

Getting Ahead of Objections

NEXT, we have to build up your confidence so you can truly believe and know that your solution is the BEST to get your prospects the outcome they are looking to receive. We'll do this by getting ahead of some objections to your "how," so when they come up, you will be able to effortlessly overcome them and they won't rattle you. Which, of course, will build your confidence in a huge way.

Many entrepreneurs have this nagging thought that pops in their mind: "Why would someone even **want** to work with me?"

Sound familiar? Yes, part of this thought has to do with your confidence, but we have to be honest about something.... your prospects are probably wondering the same thing, too! Why SHOULD they want to work with you?!

This is a normal thought process people may be going through as they are in the consideration stage of their customer journey. They are wondering whether they should work with you... or someone else. They are also debating about working with you or choosing another option entirely. They are making their best decision. And you, knowing that this is a common thought people have, can begin to overcome this challenge way ahead of time to make the sales process move much quicker so your prospects don't have to wonder for long - because, they'll just KNOW you are the clear choice for them.

We do this by focusing on YOU, first. We have to shift your thought patterns so YOU see yourself as an obvious choice first, so that you can then lead your prospects energetically to see it too, in a very natural way. When you truly believe this, they're going to believe it too. It's going to feel natural, we don't need any gimmicks or any crazy strategies. It's just going to happen naturally because you'll fully embody and believe that you are the obvious and the best choice for them. So, the way you'll communicate with your prospects will shift to subconsciously show your certainty to them, which will give them a feeling of relief and confidence in you, as well.

We've already talked about your direct competitors. Your direct competitors are people that are doing basically the same thing as you are, which is what we looked at in the previous section. Next, we want to look at alternative solutions or options that people can use or do instead of hiring you (or someone like you).

The first step is to write down the end result or outcome that your ideal clients are looking for in simple terms. What do they actually want? And remember to write what they SAY they want, not what YOU feel they need. It's about speaking their language. For example, they may say things like: "I want to find my soulmate" or "I want to lose 10 pounds." Even if YOU think that what they *actually* need (or *should* need) is to either feel more confident or love themselves. We don't really care about what you THINK they SHOULD need. It's about what they are CURRENTLY saying they want. Write that down first.

Step two is to identify at least five alternative ways people *think* they can use or do to achieve the same result they are looking for. So what else could this person do in order to achieve this result? And again, I'm not talking about working with a direct competitor, I'm talking about totally different options here.

If you are helping people lose weight, they can work with you (or someone else).... or they can join a gym, they can sign up for a group bootcamp class, they can try a new diet by reading a book, they can buy supplements, or something else. So come up with these different ways for them to potentially achieve that same result that you provide.

Once you've outlined the five alternative ways, step three is to write down some reasons as to why someone should NOT use that specific alternative option. For example, if your prospect wants to lose weight, joining a gym may not be a good fit (on its own) because most people won't go consistently and even if they do, they usually don't do the necessary things to help them lose weight and they end up wasting money and time. Or, if they wanted to get diet pills, this is also not a good idea because diet pills don't work and even worse, they can come with terrible side effects.

Step four is to write down why your product or service is better in achieving the solution than the alternative option. Why should they choose your service instead? Why is it better? Once you've outlined these, I really want you to feel into it... and really, *really* believe it. Why is your option better? Why is working with you better than them signing up for a gym and that's it? Really get clear on that. Write that down and **really** feel into that. Really allow yourself to experience a shift and belief for yourself as well.

And I know, you might be reading this and thinking that, "Well, it really depends. Some people can totally get their desired results by just joining a gym or going on a diet." I get it. I totally understand. Some options work better for some people and some options don't. But for this exercise, I really want you to do this so that you truly believe and feel that your solution is the best option for that right person. I want you to assume that, in this example, we are talking about the ideal client that you can actually help, not just some random Joe Schmo that's the average person, not exactly your ideal client. When doing this exercise, think about the ideal person that you **know** you can help. They WOULD get great results from your solution. We want them to know that. So write why your option is better than the alternatives for each.

Now step five is an addition, a little bonus, because you probably forgot about one important alternative solution that people think they can take, which is.... *taking no action at all.* And the truth is? Most people will take this route. They will think that their problems will probably just solve themselves on their own. They'll think they can just watch what they eat a little bit more and lose those 10 lbs. Or they'll just do it later. They aren't committed enough. They just keep procrastinating on it and they're not taking any action. They're hoping it solves itself. And then, of course, they don't really do it and they don't end up getting the result at all. So, you want to also write down what may happen if your ideal clients don't use your solution or use ANY of the alternatives. I want you to identify: what is the worst thing that can happen? What's the thing that they're actually afraid is going to happen if they stay where they are? By the way, if you feel uncomfortable talking about them not taking action on YOUR specific program, you can also write about it from the perspective of what will happen if they don't take ANY action at all, on any of the alternative solutions we outlined earlier. Or, what will happen if they don't hire ANY coach/service provider, not just you. I want you to really write this out and really identify this. You're going to feel a shift in yourself, in the belief as to why your service is better than not taking any action at all. Because if you're feeling like, "Oh, whatever, yeah, I guess they don't *have to* take any action. It's not really going to be that big of a deal." Do you really think you're going to be able to sell your products and services in a powerful, effective, and emotionally engaged way? No! Because YOU aren't convinced they need your service yet! This exercise will help to amplify YOUR commitment to your own service - not just theirs. So you want to make sure you get really clear on the pain they may feel. You have to really believe that each person you talk to is at the end of their rope here and the alternative is gonna really suck. If they don't change their life, they're going to be unhappy or they're going to feel miserable or whatever.

Now, as a reminder, this is an exercise for YOU. This content we're outlining here is to educate YOU and give YOU the confidence to shift your energy and mindset so you can sell your offers more effectively. While you may use some of the content we've outlined here in your messaging, that last part I personally prefer to NOT use in my marketing because I am not a proponent of fear-based marketing or the whole "stick the knife and twist it until you bleed out" type of marketing.

I personally don't focus on showing the pain that hardcore in my marketing and messaging. Twisting the knife is actually a very common, and a very effective, persuasion technique when it comes to copywriting, marketing and sales. However, I don't find it to be very heart-centered and it feels a little bit manipulative to me. So, I don't get into the pain and the negatives as hard as other sales trainers or business coaches may teach you to, however it's important to talk about challenges and struggles people experience, and it's important that you are clear on them for yourself. But I'm not gonna throw salt at the wound just to make them feel crappier. That's just doesn't feel right to me. So, in short, you have to find the right balance for you.

With that said, you still need to feel that this scary outcome is what is potentially possible for them, and what could be an outcome of not taking any action at all. This way you can start to fully get behind your offer and truly believe how it can really change your client's life. And if you don't feel it, you will have a harder time actually selling it, because you aren't really sold on it yourself. So it's really important that you go through this process and when you feel into all of these fully, you'll begin to believe that your offer can truly transform your person's life or at least improve it, and therefore you will show up a lot more powerfully in your marketing and your content. You will stand for your client in a much more significant and reliable way. You will lead them and you will call them to action much more powerfully so that they're actually going to feel empowered to work with you, because *you* believe in your solution with all of your heart. You believe that they are going to get the result that they're looking for.

Knowing all of this will make you are more prepared than 99% of your competitors. You'll also have a deeper sense of confidence and urgency when you start selling your services and you'll therefore get better results. You will also get new content ideas to share with your followers. You will get to empower people to stand up for themselves by leading the path and being their light. And lastly, you will truly see why you are the clear choice. If you don't feel like you're the clear choice, go deeper into these exercises again. You should be feeling this pretty strongly as you go through this.

17

HOW TO FOLLOW UP WITH PROSPECTS (WITHOUT BEING ANNOYING)

*S*o obviously doing sales conversations is important, but not all sales will happen on that first call. In fact, a big part of turning leads into clients actually happens in the follow up. My first coach would always tell me: "Fortune is in the Follow up."

And it's true! You want to make sure that you're following up with your prospects when they're not sure about taking that next step, so that they can actually make a *decision*. It is very common that you might get on the phone with somebody and they just won't give you a straight answer: it's not a yes, not a no. It's a maybe, it's an "I don't know."

This is one of the worst situation you can put yourself in because you're hopeful, you think that they might sign up with you! But in many situations, the client was actually a "no" but they just felt bad about telling you. Or maybe they're a yes, but they are just needing to overcome some mindset blocks and fears that might be stopping them from saying yes on that call. After all, taking a leap and investing can feel scary, so you want to help your ideal client see what their decision really is in their heart and help them make it. You want to make sure that you are there for them and you are actually doing your due diligence to get them to a decision. Your goal, in any sales environment, is to get your prospect to either a yes or no. Not maybe. Not I'm not sure yet. A decision.

So what's the follow up system I use?

First, I want to emphasize my recommendation is that you do try to enroll clients on a call. You want to get somebody on the phone, you have the sales conversation with them and they end up saying yes or no, right on that phone call. There's no "Send me and email with information and I'll let you know what I decide." That's literally the worst thing you can do because the conversation loses momentum and the likelihood for this person to say no increases. BUT, I understand that sometimes people need time and they might not be able to make a decision right off the bat.

If that happens, instead of hanging up and emailing them and hoping they get back to you, you set up another appointment with this person to have a follow up conversation and then on that call get them to a yes or a no.

There are two approaches I want to share here today.

Approach #1) You Got the Follow Up Call Scheduled

So if that happened, there are specific few emails that you can send afterwards. This process is very straight-forward because what we really want is for that person to show up and actually have that follow up conversation with you on the phone. The reason we stress being on the phone is because being present with someone on the phone is the easiest way to be present, connected, and overcome objections if that's what the prospective clients needs.

Your goal is to set up a follow up call to happen within one to five days after the initial conversation. The sooner, the better, because the longer a person waits, the less they're going to feel that momentum and feel excited about you and the possibilities of working together. The longer they wait, the more doubt is going to come up, the more fear is going to come up and the closer they might end up getting to a no, EVEN if they were 90% a yes.

So let's say that you have this call scheduled. What you want to do immediately after that sales call is you send a follow up email. What you're doing in that email is you're doing a recap of the call, you assure them that you enjoyed talking to them and that you are the right person to actually help them with this goal or challenge. And then state that you will give them a call again at what time and what date. Lastly, you want to share with them any assignment that you gave them to do in between the call.

This is the key: You want to give them something to do. Otherwise, getting on the call will feel really hard for some of these people, because people feel uncomfortable saying no. People also feel uncomfortable making decisions. So we want to make the follow up chat feel really light, casual, and not stressful at all. You want to make it clear to them that even if they decide not to move forward, you still want to chat with them.

So personally, I like to give my prospects a decision making tool, which is a small journaling exercise. I tell them to do it and then we will go over it on our call together.

And then, you call them on the appointed date and time, have the follow up call and then either close the client or let them go. Pretty straightforward.

Approach #2: No Follow Up Call Scheduled

But then, what if you talked to the prospective client and you didn't schedule the follow up call right on the phone? This actually happens probably most of the time when before people start working with me. And I get it. You talk to somebody, you get excited, you hang up and then you're like, "Oh crap, I don't have an answer. I don't have a yes or no. They said they're going to email me." That is not a situation you want to put yourself in, but in case it does happen, here's what you can do.

So first, immediately after the sales call, you're going to send a thank you email. Similarly to what I said in the previous section, you're just not going to say,

"Hey, we're going to meet again on this date." Instead, you add "Hey, when would be a good time for us to follow up? Would Friday at this time work for you?"

Then you want to send another follow up email. This is specifically if they did NOT respond to your thank you email, so if they did schedule a follow up call from that first email, you're good to go. You don't have to send more emails. You just show up on that follow up call and do the thing.

Now, if they didn't respond, you can send send another follow up email ideally two or three days after the original thank you email.

Your goal is to try to get them on the phone again, and you want to get them to see if they have any questions. Maybe you send them something to get them more excited about what you have to offer.

If they still haven't responded to you, you can send another email a couple of days after that to get them re-excited and asking them to get on the phone with you again to have that follow up conversation. You can position it a little bit differently saying,

"Hey, I have an idea for you/I was thinking about you. I wanted to see how this might resonate"

And you try to get them on the phone so you can have that conversation again and reconnect them to the vision and excitement that got them on the phone with you in the first place. Of course, if you will be sharing an "idea" you want to actually come up with something to share with them. This will provide value for them but also position you as someone who is really there for them and wants to help them implement the idea - and that's what you will do together when this person decides to enroll.

After that, you typically would just send one more email, which is all about "closing the file." You send this maybe a week or 10 days after the previous email. You can say something like this:

"Hi Name, I met with my team, I haven't heard from you and that typically means one of two things. It typically means that you're either not interested or you just haven't seen this email and it got lost or you forgot to respond. Tell me what you recommend for us cause I'm about to close the enrollment for this program."

Obviously you'll want to adjust the voice to fit your brand. And then after that, it's nothing. I might follow up a few months later, just to check in, but I won't be doing it to get them on the phone necessarily or to sell anything. Just to check in, maybe give them some value, and keep in contact. If they still don't respond, I just take them off my contact CRM list and move on. There are plenty more fish in the sea! Fish that want to hear from you ;-)

Keep in mind that sometimes people will not respond but they MAY end up buying in the future. So don't do anything weird, don't freak out, and remember that we're playing a bigger game here. Your goal is to grow, create a sustainable business, and you are stepping into abundance. So act like it. :-)

18

STARTING YOUR ALIGNED
GROWTH JOURNEY

*W*hat to Do Next?

You've just read the entire book - congratulations! As you probably already know, I am so passionate about helping entrepreneurs like you to launch, grow, and scale their aligned businesses so they can reach six, if not, multiple six figures in revenue by serving clients they love - and building a path to freedom. The truth is, while the path there may sound simple, it's not easy. And I would not be here today if I didn't have support from my mentors along the way.

So now, I want to invite you to get support, too. I've been working with entrepreneurs like you since 2014. Now, I've opened up some options to work with me and learn the step-by-step detailed processes and systems I teach my clients that get them crazy amazing results, so you can do the same.

The next step is to go to our Next Steps page and watch my free training on how you can start booking your first or next 10 clients without feeling guilty for charging what you deserve. You will also get a special invitation to join my signature program, Serve to Sell Launchpad.

Just go to: http://heartbehindhustle.com/ bonustraining to learn more and book your call today

If the link above does not work, it means there are no more spots available as there are a limited number of people I can work with at any given time in my programs.

I'd be honored and thrilled to see how our methodology can serve and support you in your rise, too. We look forward to speaking with you.

xoxo

Kamila

ABOUT THE AUTHOR

Kamila Gornia, founder of Heart Behind Hustle®, is the powerhouse business + marketing strategist for impact-driven entrepreneurs who are ready to skyrocket their income and impact online through heart-fueled strategies that convert. She helps them scale into six figures and show up as authorities in alignment with their vision and desires. Kamila has been seen on Forbes, Entrepreneur.com, Inc., Huffington Post, and several others.